HAL LEONARD
SAXOPHONE METHOD

AUDIO ACCESS INCLUDED

PLAYBACK+
Speed • Pitch • Balance • Loop

JAZZ SAXOPHONE: TENOR

BY DENNIS TAYLOR

T0071399

Recording Credits:
Tenor Saxophone: Dennis Taylor
Piano: Kelli Cox
Bass: John Vogt
Drums: Rick Reed

Engineered by Michael Holmes
Recorded at Hothaus Productions, Nashville, TN

A special thanks to my wife, Karen Leipziger — my editor, critic, and inspiration.

To access audio visit:
www.halleonard.com/mylibrary

Enter Code
1942-4573-7041-9041

ISBN 978-1-4234-2634-9

HAL•LEONARD®
CORPORATION
7777 W. BLUEMOUND RD. P.O. BOX 13819 MILWAUKEE, WI 53213

Visit Hal Leonard Online at
www.halleonard.com

THE BASICS

WHAT IS JAZZ?

The American music known as *jazz* is nearly impossible to define precisely. Some players cite improvisation, others emphasize swing, while many contend that jazz's harmonic structures best characterize the style. In the dictionary, jazz is defined as: "A style of music of Afro-American roots characterized by a strong rhythmic understructure, 'blue' notes, and improvisation on melody and chord structure."

Although barely a century old, jazz has fostered many subcategories, including:

- *Dixieland*—New Orleans and Chicago small-band jazz style developed in the early 1900s, characterized by group improvisation over a steady two-beat ragtime rhythm. Notable proponents include King Oliver, Louis Armstrong, Jelly Roll Morton, and Sidney Bechet.

- *Swing*—big band music of the 1930s, characterized by a long-short eighth-note (♫=♩♪) rhythmic feel. Notable proponents include the bands of Count Basie, Duke Ellington, Glenn Miller, and Benny Goodman.

- *Bebop*—a form of jazz originating in the 1940s, characterized by solo improvisations, complex rhythms, and extended harmonies. Notable proponents include Charlie Parker, Dizzy Gillespie, Thelonious Monk, and Bud Powell.

- *Cool Jazz*—a form of jazz originating in the 1950s, characterized by a subdued, ethereal approach, and experimental arrangements. Notable proponents include Miles Davis, Lennie Tristano, Gerry Mulligan, and Bill Evans.

- *Hard Bop*—derivative of bebop in the mid-to-late 1960s, characterized by relentless rhythms (often bluesy or funky), extended solos, and enhanced accompanimental roles. Notable proponents include Horace Silver, "Cannonball" Adderley, Jimmy Smith, Grant Green, and John Coltrane.

- *Free Jazz*—a form of jazz originating in the 1960s, characterized by the lack of preset chords, melody, and form, as well as by complex and often chaotic improvisations. Notable proponents include Ornette Coleman, Cecil Taylor, Albert Ayler, and, to a certain degree, John Coltrane.

- *Latin Jazz*—a form of jazz initiated as musicians from Cuba, Puerto Rico, and South America incorporated an even-eighth note feel into the existing sensibilities of American jazz. "Latin" has since become a generic term, usually meaning a derivative of bossa nova or samba, both of which are styles from Brazil. Notable proponents include Antonio Carlos Jobim, Joao Gilberto, Stan Getz, and Tito Puente.

- *Fusion (Jazz Rock)*—a combination of jazz and rock dating from the late 1960s, characterized by inventive solos, rock-like rhythms and arrangements, and high-volume, electric sounds. Notable proponents include Miles Davis, Chick Corea, John McLaughlin, the Brecker Brothers, and Pat Metheny.

John Coltrane

Sonny Rollins

Dexter Gordon

WHO'S WHO IN JAZZ TENOR SAXOPHONE

Listening is almost as much a part of learning to play jazz as practicing. In fact, much of any jazz style's sum and substance is derived from oral tradition—handed down from player to player, recording to recording. Simply put, if you want to play jazz well, a combination of practicing, playing, and listening is essential. Here are fifteen highly recommended milestone jazz recordings, listed in alphabetical order.

ARTIST	ALBUM TITLE	RECORD LABEL	STYLE
Michael Brecker	*Don't Try This at Home*	(Impulse)	contemporary
John Coltrane	*Giant Steps*	(Atlantic)	hard bop
Miles Davis (featuring John Coltrane)	*Kind of Blue*	(Columbia)	modal
Stan Getz	Getz/Gilberto	(Verve)	Latin
Dexter Gordon	*Go!*	(Blue Note)	swing
Coleman Hawkins	*Verve Jazz Masters 34*	(Verve)	swing
Joe Henderson	*Inner Urge*	(Blue Note)	hard bop
Joe Lovano	*Trio Fascination*	(Blue Note)	contemporary
Sonny Rollins	*Saxophone Colossus*	(Prestige)	hard bop
Wayne Shorter	*Speak No Evil*	(Blue Note)	hard bop
Sonny Stitt	*Tune-up*	(Muse)	bebop
Stanley Turrentine	*The Best of Stanley Turrentine: The Blue Note Years*	(Blue Note)	soul/blues
Grover Washington, Jr.,	*Mr. Magic*	(Motown)	funk/jazz
Ben Webster	*Ben Webster Meets Oscar Peterson*	(Verve)	swing
Lester Young	*Lester Young with the Oscar Peterson Trio*	(Verve)	swing

It is also recommended you listen to the following tenor sax players:

Swing: Al Cohn, Zoot Sims, Ike Quebec, Illinois Jacquet
Bebop: Don Byas, Wardell Gray, Johnny Griffin, James Moody
Hard bop: Gene Ammons, Hank Mobley, Harold Land, George Coleman
Avant garde: Pharoah Sanders, Archie Shepp, Albert Ayler, David Murray
Funk/jazz: King Curtis, Eddie Harris, Bob Berg, Bennie Maupin
Contemporary: Chris Potter, Branford Marsalis, James Carter, Bob Mintzer, Jerry Bergonzi, Eric Alexander, Joshua Redman

Lester Young

Coleman Hawkins

Joe Henderson

JAZZ PERFORMANCE ESSENTIALS

In jazz, it's very common for a group of strangers to get together to play, totally unrehearsed, on a gig in front of a live audience. As a result, there are certain terms and procedures that exist to ensure that things run smoothly.

Generally speaking, jazz songs follow a standard format: head in, solos, and head out. The term "head" refers to a tune's melody, which is played by one or more of the band's lead instruments while the rest of the band accompanies. Protocol says that once the head is played once or twice at the beginning of the piece, various soloists then improvise solos based on the chord progression (or *changes*) of the original melody. When the soloists are finished, the head is played to conclude the song.

Many songs also include intros, endings, and "trading" sections. Intros may be derived from a portion of the tune's form (often the last eight bars), a pedal on the fifth of the key, a spontaneous opening cadenza, or a specially composed part that takes the band into the head. There are several ways to end a song. Sometimes a tune has a specific coda section that provides an ending, oftentimes the last four or eight bars can be tagged or repeated to set up the end, occasionally a standard *ritard* (gradually slowing down) works, or players frequently will employ one of three or four cliché riff endings. Sometimes, usually right before the head out, musicians trade "fours" or "eights." This means that one soloist improvises over the first four (or eight) bars of the form, then another soloist improvises over the next four (or eight), and so on. There are a number of different ways to mix the trading up—probably the most common is to give the drummer every other four bars. Note that "trading" sections cover a tune's entire form, and should lead right back to the head, or top of the tune.

Structurally, most jazz tunes extend either twelve, sixteen, twenty-four, or thirty-two bars. It is important to recognize, and eventually memorize, the structure and form of the tunes you play. Musicians often refer to the first part of the form as the "A" section, and the second part as the "B" section, the "bridge," the middle section, or the "channel." Get used to keeping track of the form at all times—it is extremely important to maintain where you are at any given time in the tune.

You'll encounter many other survival situations in almost every gig you play. No book can truly prepare you for each and every encounter, but here are three things for which to watch out: 1) Be aware of who might want to solo next; 2) If you're performing with a singer, be conscious of the key and entrance habits he or she prefers; 3) Mix up the tempos from song to song.

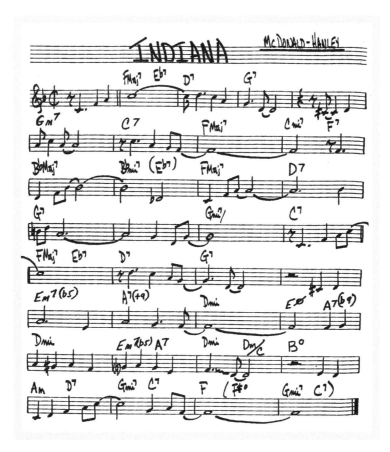

Most jazz combos read from a "lead sheet" similar to the one shown above.
A lead sheet provides the melody or "head," the changes, and the form of
the tune.

MOUTHPIECES AND REEDS

Mouthpieces

Saxophone mouthpieces can be made from a wide variety of materials: plastic, hard rubber, metal, even wood. The stock mouthpieces that come with saxophones at the time of purchase are usually made of resonite or plastic. These are inexpensive and typically designed for beginners. It is recommended that, as a student progresses, he/she switch to a hard rubber mouthpiece. This will improve tone quality and intonation. For a young student playing in a school jazz ensemble, a hard rubber mouthpiece will help with blend, pitch, and a more consistent sound within the sax section. Metal mouthpieces generally produce a brighter, edgier sound with more projection, but young students may have a difficult time controlling metal mouthpieces. A student should only move to a metal mouthpiece after he/she has been playing a while and has started to build a strong *embouchure* (position of mouth and lips).

hard rubber mouthpiece

metal mouthpiece

Reeds

In choosing reeds you'll want to match the size of the mouthpiece's tip opening with the strength of the reed: the larger the tip opening, the softer the reed; the smaller the tip opening, the harder the reed. A reed that is too stiff for your setup will result in an unfocused sound, be unresponsive and difficult to play in the low register, and cause premature embouchure fatigue. A reed that is too soft will be unresponsive as well, especially in the upper register, producing a dull, non-resonant tone, and causing intonation problems by playing flat. Through trial and error, you'll find the setup that's right for you.

Breaking in your reeds properly will enhance their durability. Soak a new reed in water for a few minutes and place it on a flat surface like a piece of glass or a reed resurfacer. Then rub the reed with your thumb from where the cut is to the tip. Doing this six to eight times will seal the fibers and help the reed to last longer. For the first two days with a new reed, play only in the soft to medium dynamic range for about five minutes per day.

To protect the reed and prevent it from warping as it dries, remove the reed from the mouthpiece after you're done playing and place it in a reed holder. After playing on a reed for a period of time (generally a week or more) the backside will start to warp. Rub the backside of the reed with light sandpaper or a reed resurfacer. This will help bring the reed back to life. A reed clipper will also help reeds last longer: as a reed gets softer, clip just a tiny amount off the tip.

reed

reed clipper

SWING ARTICULATION

Each saxophonist's style of articulation is as unique as his or her sound. The best teachers are in your collection of recordings.

The following exercises will help you develop your jazz tonguing technique while practicing major scales. Try tonguing the upbeats lightly and slurring into the downbeats. This approach will help you produce lines of clarity and forward motion. Be careful not to clip off the sound of the note on the downbeat. Keep blowing a constant air stream for the entire phrase. As the tempo increases, try including more notes under each slur.

In Exercise 1, set the metronome to click on beats 2 and 4, and play through all major scales using this articulation. As you increase the tempo, switch to the articulation in Exercise 2. Remember to phrase your eighth notes with a good strong swing feel.

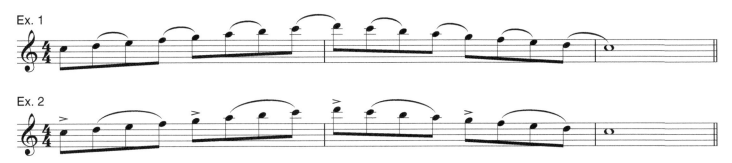

MAXIMIZING YOUR SOUND

Aural Concept

To develop your tone, it is important to have a concept in mind of what you want to sound like. Find someone whose sound you love and make him or her your musical model. Try to approximate that sound on your sax. Listen to recordings, then play along with them. You might begin with just a short phrase: listen to the phrase; stop the recording; then try to capture all the nuances of the sound. As you get inside the sound of your favorite player, you will start to develop the physical capacity to produce that tone. As you grow, your aural concept will evolve into a combination of all the people whose music you love and have absorbed. Then, your own personality and musical voice will emerge.

Practice Small to Be Big

Set aside time in every practice session to play as softly as possible, yet with a good clear tone. The longer you can do this, the better. It is easy to play loudly, but it is difficult to play loudly with a tone that is large, focused, strong, and rounded. Playing softly uses an entirely different set of muscles in your embouchure. Strengthening these muscles will help you get a full sound with lots of projection, at any volume level.

A good exercise for this is adapted from a brass exercise:

> Start on low F and begin the note with air, no tongue. Play in the *mp–mf* range. Hold for fifteen to twenty seconds. Normally, when inhaling you want to breathe through the nose and corners of the mouth simultaneously. But for this exercise, breathe in slowly only through the nose, keeping the corners of your mouth flexed around the mouthpiece. Then, play the same note an octave higher, listening carefully to the pitch, again holding for fifteen to twenty seconds. Drop back down to F♯ and repeat. Play through the "burn," never relaxing your embouchure. When your chops are aching, then release. Play this exercise in all registers of your instrument.

Train Sound

Another tone-development exercise is the "train sound." Begin on low G with lots of diaphragm support and keep your throat open. Set the metronome to ♩ = 60, and play four whole notes tied together. Begin the note with air (no tongue), and crescendo evenly through the first eight beats. The loudest point will be beat 9 (beat 1 of the third whole note). Then gradually get softer all the way back to a whisper. The effect, when done properly, is like that of a train off in the distance that approaches steadily, is in front of you on beat 9, then fades away.

CHORDS

One of the distinctive characteristics of jazz is its harmony, or chords. In contrast to most pop, rock, folk, and country songs (which use mainly three-note chords, such as major and minor triads), virtually all forms of jazz use chords that contain four or more different notes (seventh chords, extended chords, and altered chords). In addition, jazz progressions frequently contain many different chords, and often travel through multiple key centers.

SEVENTH CHORDS

A seventh chord is comprised of four notes: the three notes of a triad plus a major, minor, or diminished seventh. For instance, if you begin with the C major triad and add a major seventh (B), a C major seventh chord is formed. Likewise, if you substitute the minor (or flatted) seventh (B♭) for the B, you have a new seventh chord, C7, also known as a C dominant seventh chord.

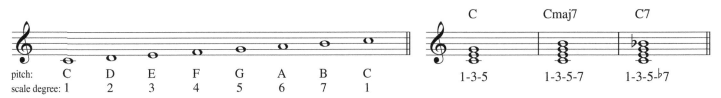

As with triads, seventh chords come in many types, including major, minor, diminished, augmented, suspended, and others. Following is a list of seventh-chord types and their constructions.

CHORD TYPE	FORMULA	NOTES (C AS ROOT)	CHORD NAME
major seventh	1–3–5–7	C–E–G–B	Cmaj7, CM7, Cma7, C△7
dominant seventh	1–3–5–♭7	C–E–G–B♭	C7, Cdom7
minor seventh	1–♭3–5–♭7	C–E♭–G–B♭	Cm7, Cmin7, C-7
minor seven flat five (half-diminished seventh)	1–♭3–♭5–♭7	C–E♭–G♭–B♭	Cm7♭5, Cø7
diminished seventh	1–♭3–♭5–♭♭7	C–E♭–G♭–B♭♭(A)	C°7, Cdim7
augmented seventh	1–3–♯5–♭7	C–E–G♯–B♭	C+7, C7♯5, Caug7
dominant seven flat five	1–3–♭5–♭7	C–E–G♭–B♭	C7♭5, C7(-5)
minor/major seventh	1–♭3–5–7	C–E♭–G–B	Cm(maj7), C-(maj7)

The following exercises will help you become more familiar with the five most common chord types. Practice each pattern in multiple keys.

Exercise 3 takes you through the major seventh, dominant seventh, minor seventh, minor seventh/flatted fifth, and diminished seventh by changing one note at a time. Exercise 4 stretches the previous pattern over two octaves. Exercise 5 begins each chord with its third; Exercise 6 begins each chord with its fifth; and Exercise 7 begins each chord with its seventh.

F°7

Ex. 4   Cmaj7   C7

Cm7   Cm7♭5

C°7

Ex. 5   Fmaj7   F7

Fm7   Fm7♭5

F°7

Ex. 6   Fmaj7   F7

Fm7   Fm7♭5

F°7

Ex. 7   Fmaj7   F7

Fm7   Fm7♭5

F°7

Play the seventh chords (in root position) to the following chord progressions. Memorize the formula for building each chord. Be conscious of the notes and the sound—don't just blindly push keys. Try singing the pitches and learn to hear the sound of each chord.

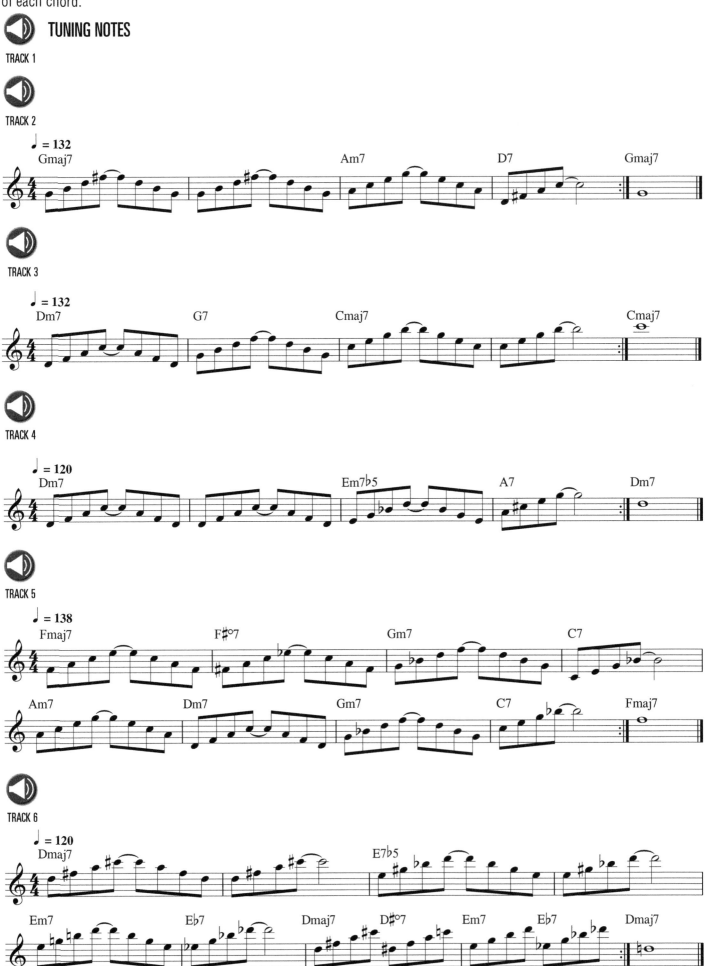

A good way to learn new songs is to play the chords (in root position) to any of the standards in your fake book. Write them out only if you have to.

EXTENDED CHORDS

Extended chords are those that include notes beyond the seventh scale degree. For example, if you take a C dominant seventh chord and add a major ninth (D), you get a C dominant ninth chord (C–E–G–Bb–D). Extended chords include ninth, eleventh, and thirteenth chords. These chords have a rich, complex sound that is well-suited for jazz. Following is a list of extended chords and their constructions.

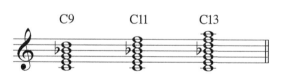

CHORD TYPE	FORMULA	NOTES (C AS ROOT)	CHORD NAME
major ninth	1–3–5–7–9	C–E–G–B–D	Cmaj9, CM9, Cma9, C△9
dominant ninth	1–3–5–b7–9	C–E–G–Bb–D	C9, Cdom9
minor ninth	1–b3–5–b7–9	C–Eb–G–Bb–D	Cm9, Cmin9, C-9
dominant eleventh	1–3–5–b7–9–11	C–E–G–Bb–D–F	C11, Cdom11
minor eleventh	1–b3–5–b7–9–11	C–Eb–G–Bb–D–F	Cm11, Cmin11, C-11
major thirteenth	1–3–5–7–9–11–13	C–E–G–B–D–F–A	Cmaj13, CM13, C△13
dominant thirteenth	1–3–5–b7–9–11–13	C–E–G–bB–D–F–A	C13, Cdom13
minor thirteenth	1–b3–5–b7–11–13	C–Eb–G–bB–D–F–A	Cm13, Cmin13, C-13

You will not likely come across a major eleventh chord*; the dissonance produced by the major third against the eleventh sounds rather unpleasant. For the same reason, the eleventh degree is routinely omitted from major thirteenth chords.

Exercises 8–10 introduce various extensions, one-by-one, to seventh chords.

Ex. 8

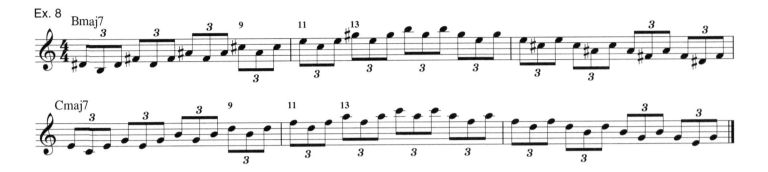

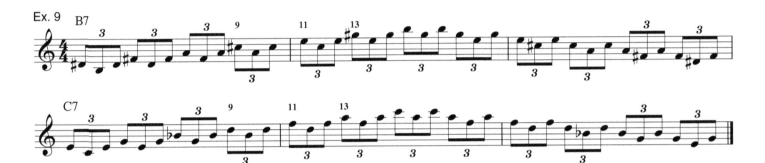

Ex. 9

Ex. 10

---

* In almost all instances, a major nine sharp eleventh (an altered chord—see pp. 14–16) will be used instead.

Now try some progressions that use extended chords.

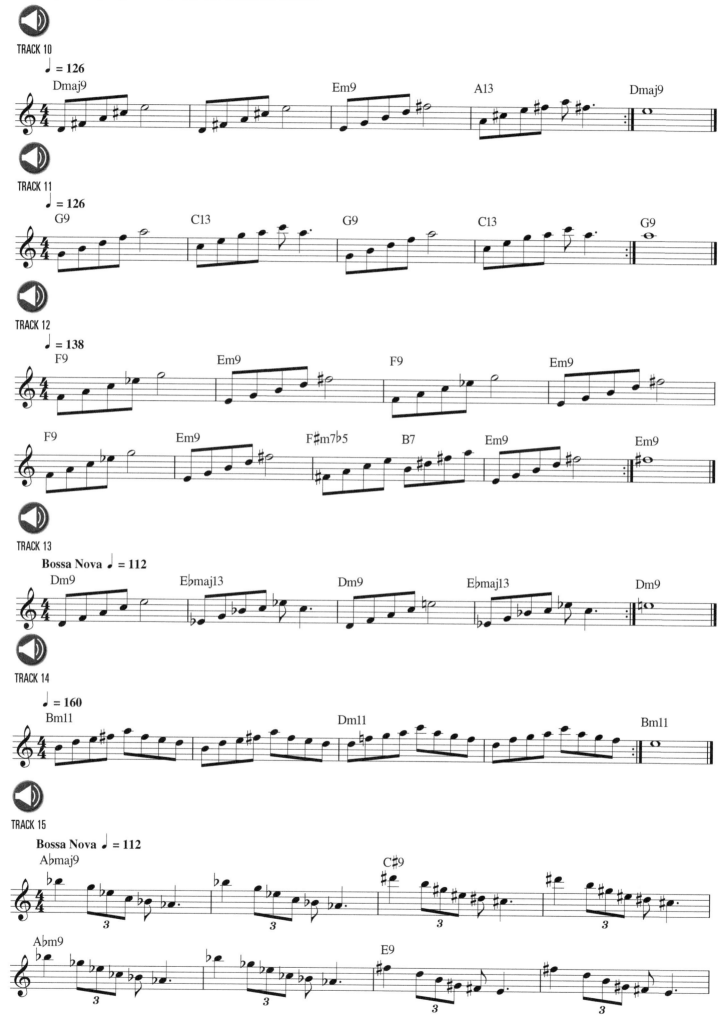

ALTERED CHORDS

An *altered chord* contains one or more notes that have been raised or lowered chromatically. The altered notes are usually the fifth, ninth, eleventh, or thirteenth.

Following is a list of altered chords and their constructions.

CHORD TYPE	FORMULA	NOTES (C AS ROOT)	CHORD NAME
dominant seven, flat five	1–3–♭5–♭7	C–E–G♭–B♭	C7♭5, C7(-5)
dominant seven, sharp five (a.k.a. aumented seventh)	1–3–♯5–♭7	C–E–G♯–B♭	C⁺7, C7♯5, Caug7
dominant seven, flat nine	1–3–5–♭7–♭9	C–E–G–B♭–D♭	C7♭9, C7(-9)
dominant seven, sharp nine	1–3–5–♭7–♯9	C–E–G–B♭–D♯	C7♯9, C7(+9)
dominant seven, flat five, flat nine	1–3–♭5–♭7–♭9	C–E–G♭–B♭–D♭	C7♭9♭5, C7♭5(♭9), C7(♭9-5)
dominant seven, sharp five, sharp nine	1–3–♯5–♭7–♯9	C–E–G♯–B♭–D♯	C7♯9♯5, C⁺7♯9, C7♯5(♯9)
dominant seven, flat five, sharp nine	1–3–♭5–♭7–♯9	C–E–G♭–B♭–D♯	C7♯9♭5, C7♭5(♯9)
dominant seven, sharp five, flat nine	1–3–♯5–♭7–♭9	C–E–G♯–♭B–D♭	C7♭9♯5, C⁺7♭9, C7♯5(♭9)
dominant seven, sharp eleven	1–3–5–♭7–♯11	C–E–G–B♭–F♯	C7♯11, C7(+11)
dominant nine, flat five	1–3–♭5–♭7–9	C–E–G♭–B♭–D	C9♭5, C9(-5)
dominant nine, sharp five	1–3–♯5–♭7–9	C–E–G♯–B♭–D	C9♯5, C⁺9, C9(+5)
dominant nine, sharp eleven	1–3–5–♭7–9–♯11	C–E–G–B♭–D–F♯	C9♯11, C9(+11)
dominant thirteen, flat nine	1–3–5–♭7–♭9–11–13	C–E–G–B♭–D♭–F–A	C13♭9, C13(-9)
dominant thirteen, sharp nine	1–3–5–♭7–♯9–11–13	C–E–G–B♭–D♯–F–A	C13♯9, C13(+9)
dominant thirteen, sharp eleven	1–3–5–♭7–9–♯11–13	C–E–G–B♭–D–F♯–A	C13♯11, C13(+11)
minor seven, flat five (a.k.a. half diminished seventh)	1–♭3–♭5–♭7	C–E♭–G♭–B♭	Cm7♭5, C-7♭5, Cø7
minor seven, sharp five	1–♭3–♯5–♭7	C–E♭–G♯–B♭	Cm7♯5, C-7♯5
major seven, flat five	1–3–♭5–7	C–E–G♭–B	Cm7♭5, CM7♭5, C△7♭5
major seven, sharp five	1–3–♯5–7	C–E–G♯–B	Cmaj7♯5, CM7♯5, C△7♯5
major seven, sharp eleven	1–3–5–7–♯11	C–E–G–B–F♯	Cmaj7♯11, CM7♯11, C△7♯11
major nine, sharp eleven	1–3–5–7–9–♯11	C–E–G–B–D–F♯	Cmaj9♯11, CM9♯11, C△9♯11

Now practice some progressions using altered chords.

TRACK 16

OTHER COMMON CHORDS

Below are some additional frequently used jazz chords.

The Sixth Chord

The *sixth* chord is created by adding a sixth to a major triad. This is the equivalent of stacking a major 2nd on top of the triad (above the fifth). The sixth chord is a good substitute for the major seventh, especially if the root is in the melody. It is also used to create motion by alternating with the major seventh chord in situations where the same major chord is played for a considerable length of time.

The Minor Sixth Chord

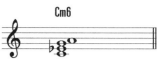

The *minor sixth* chord is created by adding a sixth to a minor triad. It has a dark, bitter sound. The minor sixth chord is a good substitute chord for the minor seventh. It is also used to create motion by alternating with the minor seventh chord in situations where the same minor chord is played for a considerable length of time.

The Six-Nine Chord

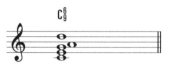

The *six-nine* chord is created by adding a sixth and ninth to a major triad. The seventh is not included. The six-nine chord is a colorful substitute for the major seventh.

Sus Chords

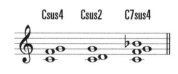

Sus chords replace the third of a chord with the fourth, as in "sus4," or sometimes with the second, as in "sus2" (pronounced "suss four" and "suss two"—the abbreviation "sus" is short for "suspended"). The resulting sound is incomplete or unresolved and has an interesting quality that is neither major nor minor. The *suspended seventh* chord is made up of the 1st, 4th, 5th, and ♭7th scale degrees. It is often used as a substitute for the dominant eleventh.

Add Chords

An *add* chord is simply a basic triad (such as a major chord) to which an extra note is added. For example, if you take a C chord and add a D to it, you have a *Cadd2* chord (with the notes C–D–E–G). This chord is different than Csus2, which has no E. Add chords are typically used more in a contemporary jazz settings than in traditional jazz.

Slash Chords

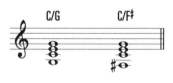

Sometimes a chord symbol includes a slash mark (/) and an extra letter, like this: *C/G* (pronounced "C over G"). *Slash* chords are used to specify a bass note other than the root of the chord. To the left of the slash is the chord itself; to the right of the slash is the bass note for that chord. Often, these bass notes are tones of the chord, such as a third, a fifth, or a seventh, though they may be notes outside the chord instead. C/F♯, for instance, would be a polychord that contains a bass note not otherwise belonging to the chord.

Slash chords are generally only necessary if the note in the bass is particularly important—if it belongs to a descending bass line, for instance—or if the note does not normally belong in the chord and is necessary for the overall sound.

CHORD TYPE	FORMULA	NOTES (C AS ROOT)	CHORD NAME
sixth	1–3–5–6	C–E–G–A	C6
minor sixth	1–♭3–5–6	C–E♭–G–A	Cm6, C–6
sixth, added ninth	1–3–5–6–9	C–E–G–A–D	C6/9, C$^6_9$
suspended second	1–2–5	C–D–G	Csus2
suspended fourth	1–4–5	C–F–G	Csus4, Csus
dominant seventh, suspended fourth	1–4–5–♭7	C–F–G–B♭	C7sus4, C7sus
added ninth	1–3–5–9	C–E–G–D	Cadd9, C(add9)
minor, added ninth	1–♭3–5–9	C–E♭–G–D	Cm(add9)

Now try applying the chords you just learned to some common jazz progressions.

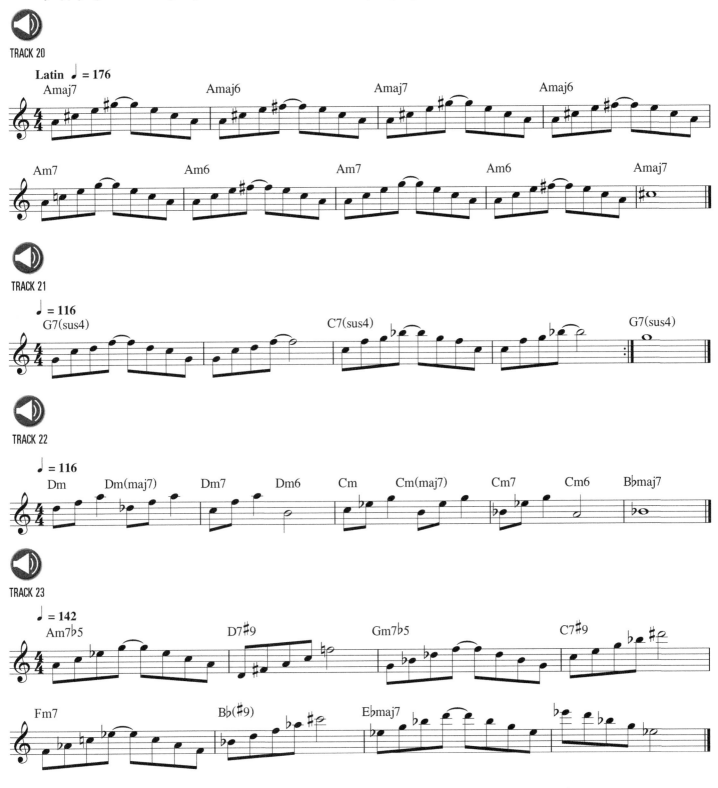

VOICE LEADING

Voice leading refers to moving smoothly from chord to chord, usually by a half or whole step. This will help give your improvised lines continuity, and enable you to move through the chord changes more easily. The most important tones of each chord are the third and the seventh, for they determine the quality of the chord (major, minor, dominant, etc.).

In Exercise 11, the seventh of each minor chord resolves down by half step to the third of the next dominant chord.

In Exercise 12, the third of each minor chord becomes the seventh of the subsequent dominant chord.

Exercise 13 uses "7–3–7" voice leading through a four-bar ii–V–I progression.

Exercise 14 demonstrates "3–7–3" voice leading in a ii–V–I progression.

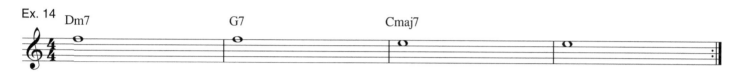

Exercise 15 is a lick that stresses important notes of each chord, voice leading through the progression.

Exercises 16 and 17 are ii–V exercises that don't resolve to the I chord.

Exercises 18 and 19 are ii–V exercises, this time using a ♭9 on the dominant chord to lead into the next chord.

Ex. 18

Practice using the voice-leading concepts you just learned to play the following examples with the audio. Begin by playing the patterns from Exercises 13–15 over the changing harmonies of Track 24. Then move to the more elaborate voice leading passages of Tracks 25–27.

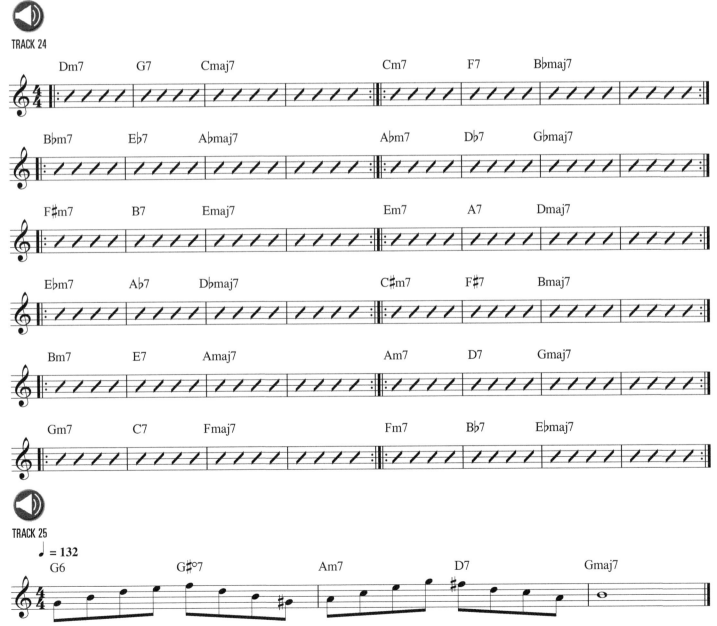

*CIRCLE OF 5THS

The *circle of 5ths* is a useful tool if you want to visualize keys and practice moving through consecutive ii–V progressions. Going counter-clockwise takes you through the major keys in ascending perfect 4ths: C–F–B♭–E♭–A♭–D♭–etc. Moving in the same direction also allows you to practice consecutive ii–V progressions. For example, you could play Cm7–F7, Fm7–B♭7, B♭m7–E♭7, E♭m7–A♭7, and so on. You could even extend these progressions to ii–V–I: for example, playing Cm7–F7–B♭maj7, Fm7–B♭7–E♭maj7, etc.

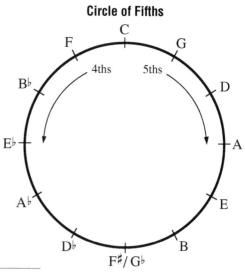

Circle of Fifths

*Note: The terms "circle of 5ths," "circle of 4ths," "cycle of 5ths," and "cycle of 4ths" are all synonymous.

The following nine exercises demonstrate playing in the circle of 5ths.

Exercise 20 runs degrees 1–2–3–5 of the major scale, moving through the circle of 5ths. Exercise 21 runs degrees 1–2–3–5 of the minor scale, moving through the circle of 5ths. Exercise 22 combines the minor and major 1–2–3–5, so we now have a iim7–V7 progression through the circle of 5ths.

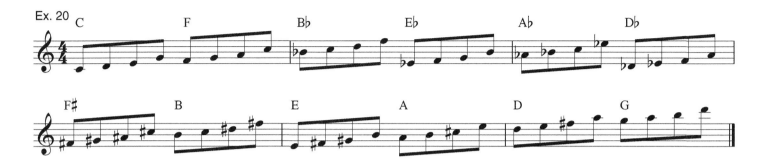

Exercise 23 is a two-measure pattern in major, run through the cycle. Exercise 24 converts this two-measure pattern to minor, then runs it through the same cycle.

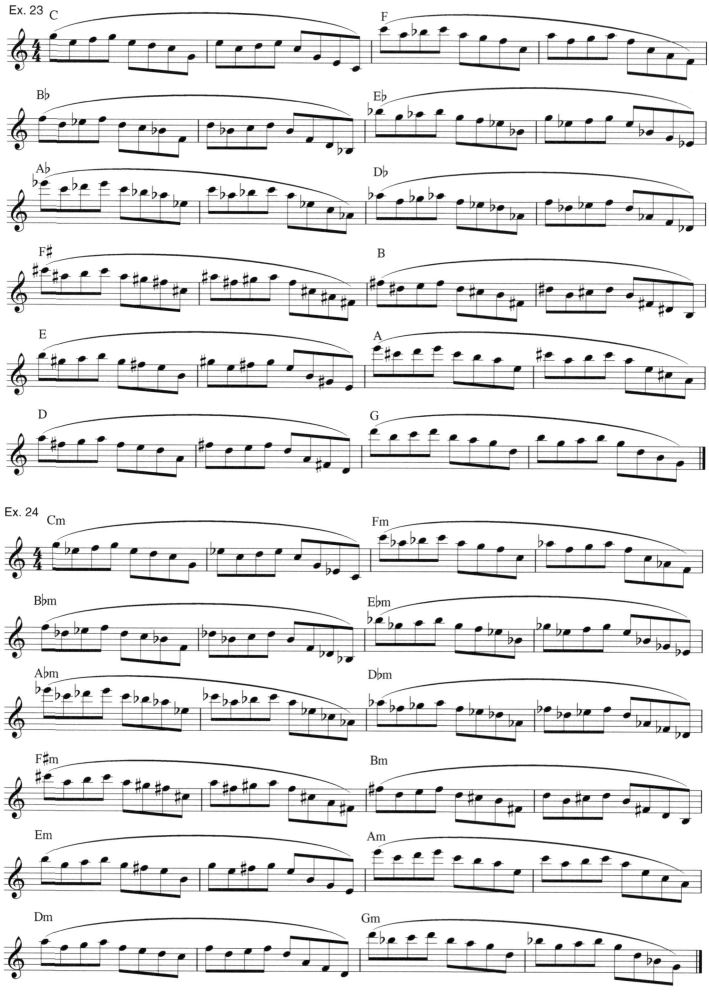

Exercise 25 features a sequence moving around the circle of 5ths. Each new chord is approached from a half step above, resulting in lines sounding similar to those performed by a bass player. Familiarity with this exercise will help the improviser hear ahead of the changes.

Ex. 25

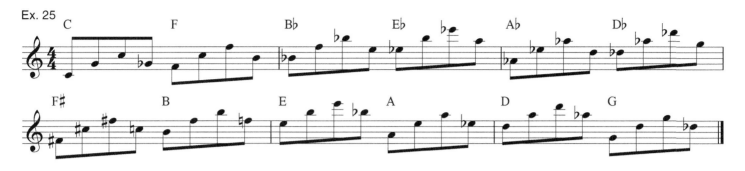

Exercise 26 presents a pattern in major. After playing it in major, change it to minor using only your ear—don't write it out.

Ex. 26

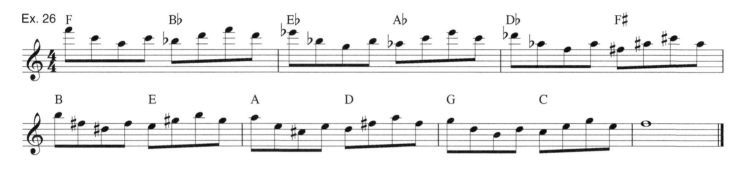

Exercises 27 and 28 explore dominant seventh/flatted ninth chords in the circle of 5ths.

Ex. 27

Ex. 28

COMMON CHORD PROGRESSIONS

It's one thing to know the chords, but it's another thing to understand their functionality. Jazz compositions can appear very complex at first. However, they can often be reduced to logical chord movements and recognizable formulas.

The ii-V

The most important progression in jazz is a minor seventh chord resolving up a 4th or down a 5th to a dominant seventh chord. This progression is known as the *ii-V progression*. The Roman numerals identify the chords' relationship to the key:

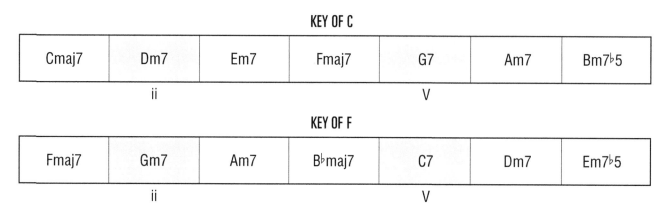

KEY OF C

Cmaj7	Dm7	Em7	Fmaj7	G7	Am7	Bm7♭5
	ii			V		

KEY OF F

Fmaj7	Gm7	Am7	B♭maj7	C7	Dm7	Em7♭5
	ii			V		

The ii-V progression can also be found in minor keys:

KEY OF C MINOR

Cm(maj7)	Dm7♭5	E♭maj7♯5	Fm7	G7	A♭maj7	B°7
	ii			V		

KEY OF F MINOR

Fm(maj7)	Gm7♭5	A♭maj7♯5	B♭m7	C7	D♭maj7	E°7
	ii			V		

Almost all jazz compositions employ various ii–V progressions. Following are several typical chord patterns. The symbols underneath the staff provide a measure-by-measure analysis of the key from which each chord comes. The letter before the colon indicates the key, and the Roman numeral identifies the chord's relationship to that key.

TRACK 28

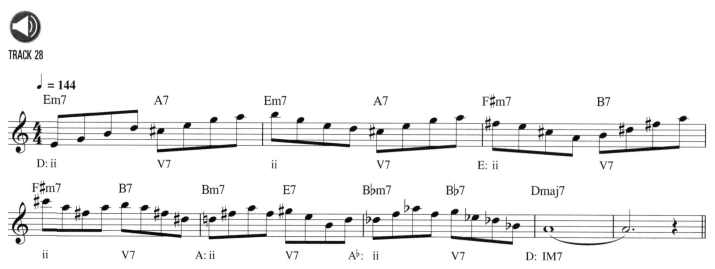

24

Notice how these examples are starting to sound like solos. Write your own solos using chord tones, and remember: leave space; vary the rhythms; start phrases on upbeats to give your lines forward motion; explore the entire range of the saxophone.

IMPROVISATION

At the heart of jazz is *improvisation*, the spontaneous expression of musical ideas. Most jazz songs offer space for musicians to showcase their abilities to ad-lib solos.

Improvisers develop their unique voices through personal quirks of tone and timing. Thus, both note-choice and phrasing play key roles in how interesting an improvised statement is. Listening to great saxophonists like Charlie Parker, Coleman Hawkins, John Coltrane, and Sonny Rollins is invaluable. Furthermore, studying lines from other jazz instrumentalists is important to a full understanding of the idiom.

As clichéd as it might sound, playing a solo is like telling a story. In order to convey a good story, you need to know what you're talking about. This means you must know the chords over which you'll be improvising, as well as the scales that correspond to them. A *scale* is a series of notes arranged in a specific order or pattern. For every chord, there is at least one scale that works well for improvisation. Jazz music makes use of many different scales, including the major scale (and its modes), the harmonic minor scale, the melodic minor scale, the diminished scale, the whole tone scale, and others. Understanding the construction of these scales, and their relationship to chords is crucial. The following pages explain these basic relationships in detail.

THE MAJOR SCALE

The most common scale is the *major scale*. It's the basis of countless melodies, riffs, solos, and chord progressions.

Construction

Scales are constructed using a combination of whole steps and half steps. All major scales are built from the following step pattern.

WHOLE – WHOLE – HALF – WHOLE – WHOLE – WHOLE – HALF

This series of whole and half steps gives the major scale its characteristic sound. To build a C major scale, start with the note C and follow the step pattern above.

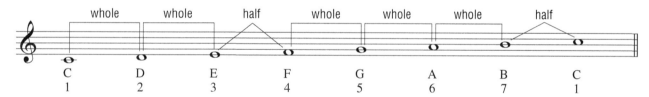

The first degree of a major scale is called the *tonic*. This is the "home" tone on which most melodies end.

To build a G major scale, start with the note G and apply the major-scale step pattern.

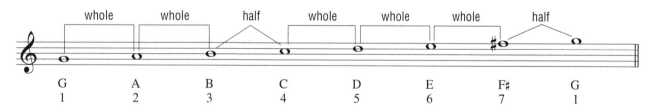

The major scale step pattern can be applied to any starting note to create any major scale. If you start on D, you will have a D major scale: D-E-F#-G-A-B-C#-D. If you start on E, you will have an E major scale: E-F#-G#-A-B-C#-D#-E. If you start on F, you will have an F major scale, and so on.

Major-Scale Exercises

It's important to know your major scales inside and out, and to be able to play those scales throughout the entire range of the saxophone. Tonal areas often shift quickly in jazz, so having the technique to move rapidly from key to key is very important.

In Exercise 29, the C major scale is played from the tonic (C), to the highest (F) and lowest (B) notes of the scale that are within the normal range of the saxophone, then back to the tonic. Work on being able to play all major scales this way. Strive for a consistently full sound from bottom to top.

Ex. 29

In Exercise 30 the F major scale is played up through one octave, resolving down a half step to a descending E major scale, which then moves down another half step to an ascending E♭ major scale, and so on. This is designed to give the feeling of playing through chord changes.

Ex. 30

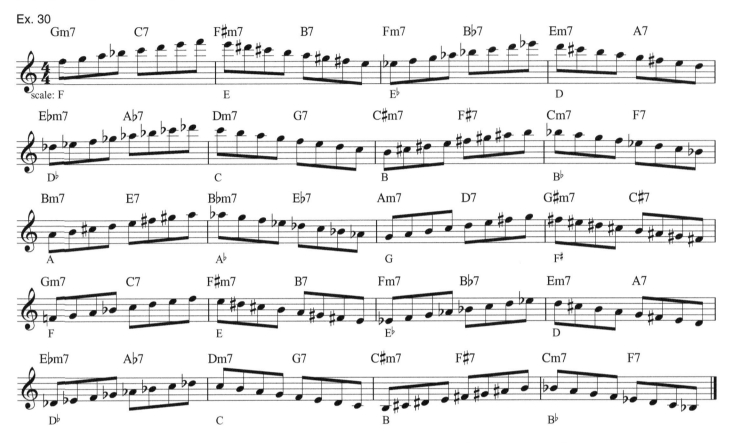

Exercise 31 is the same type of exercise working up from the bottom of the sax through every major key.

Ex. 31

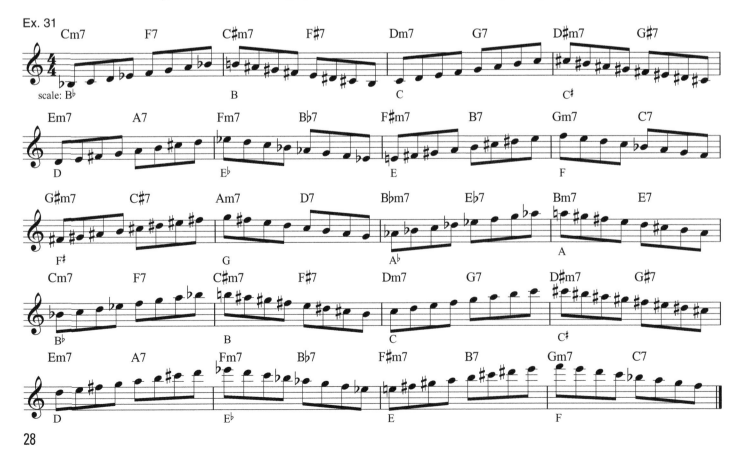

Chords of the Major Scale

Chords and chord progressions are also derived from scales. A piece of music based on the C major scale is in the key of C major. For every key, there are seven corresponding chords—one built on each degree of the major scale.

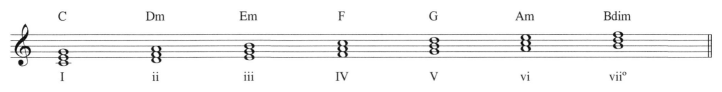

In taking a closer look at each of the seven chords, you will notice that major triads are built on the 1st, 4th, and 5th degrees of the scale; minor triads are built on the 2nd, 3rd, and 6th degrees of the scale; and a diminished triad is built on the 7th degree. The seven chords are common to the key of C because all seven contain only the notes of the C major scale. It is important to memorize this sequence of chord types, as it applies to all major scales.

Exercise 32 runs a triplet pattern through all seven triads of the C major scale.

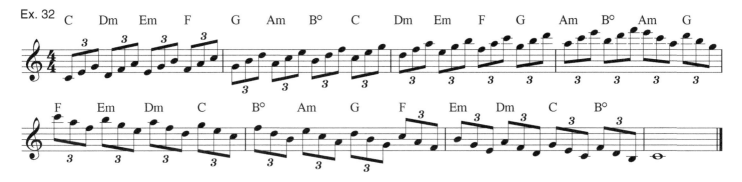

Of course, most jazz chord progressions contain seventh chords instead of triads. The seventh chords built on the degrees of the C major scale are:

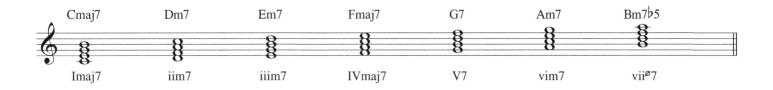

Exercises 33 and 34 demonstrate the seventh chords available in C major.

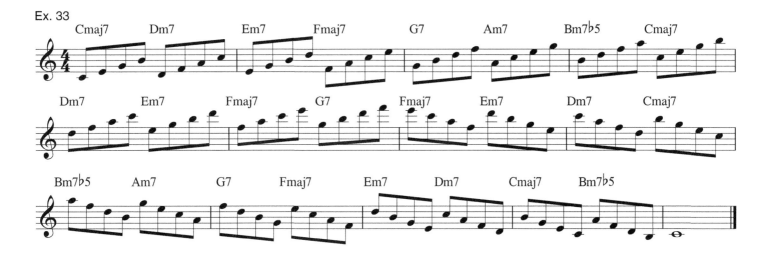

29

Ex. 34

The secret to applying scales effectively to chords is knowing how chords can be grouped together so that one scale can be used to improvise over a series of chord "changes." Most jazz compositions pass through multiple keys; however, through an understanding of the chord-scale relationships introduced above, it often becomes possible to organize a few consecutive chords into one tonal center. This will enable you to improvise over these chords without needing to change scales.

Track 34 plays a chord progression in the key of C. Over the track, first play up and down the C major scale to notice how the notes work over the chords, as shown in Exercise 35. Later, try to mix-up the notes, as demonstrated in Exercises 36 and 37.

The progression in Track 35 is also in the key of C; yet this is disguised slightly by the presence of extended chords. Extended chords function in keeping with the chord family from which they are derived. For example, a Cmaj9 chord is an extension of C. Similarly, G9, G11, and G13 are all part of the dominant chord family, and function in the same way that a plain G7 chord would. You can improvise over the progression using the C major scale. Try to emphasize the extensions, as demonstrated in Exercise 38.

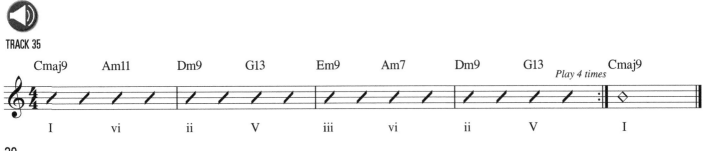

Ex. 38

IMPROVISATION TIPS

- **Cling to the Chords** – Emphasize the notes of each chord being played.

- **Less is More** – Choose your notes carefully; sometimes it's not the quantity but the quality. Adding spaces (rests) is also helpful.

- **Work the Rhythm** – Use syncopation, triplets, and repeating patterns to help make your solos interesting and distinctive.

- **Tell a Story** – Let your solo take shape with a beginning, middle, and end.

MODES OF THE MAJOR SCALE

Modes are scales built upon different notes of a parent scale. Just as there are seven notes in a major scale, there are seven modes derived from the major scale. The names of these seven modes are: Ionian, Dorian, Phrygian, Lydian, Mixolydian, Aeolian, and Locrian. It's important to point out that each of these modes is just a permuted major scale. That is, the seven modes of C major all contain the same notes; they just start and end in different places.

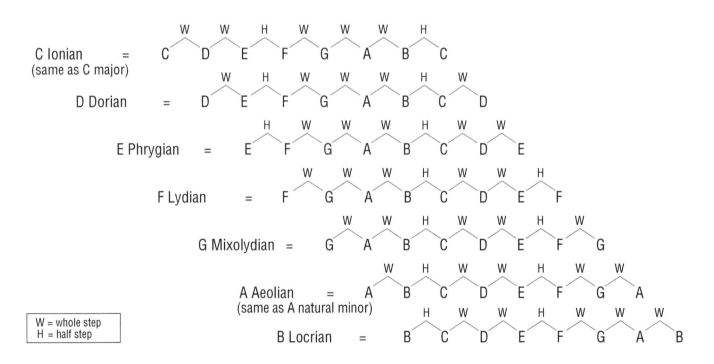

Each mode of the major scale corresponds to the diatonic chord that shares the same root. The C Ionian mode could be used to improvise over Cmaj7, the G Mixolydian mode would be used over G7, the V chord of C major, and so on. You might ask, "Aren't these modes the same as the major scale we just learned?" The answer is yes; it's just the terminology that differs. When you see a chord progression that travels from Dm7 to G7 to Cmaj7, you can think of playing C major, or you can think of playing D Dorian to G Mixolydian to C Ionian. Thinking modally simply puts more emphasis on the starting note.

Exercise 39 shows the seven modes of the C major scale.

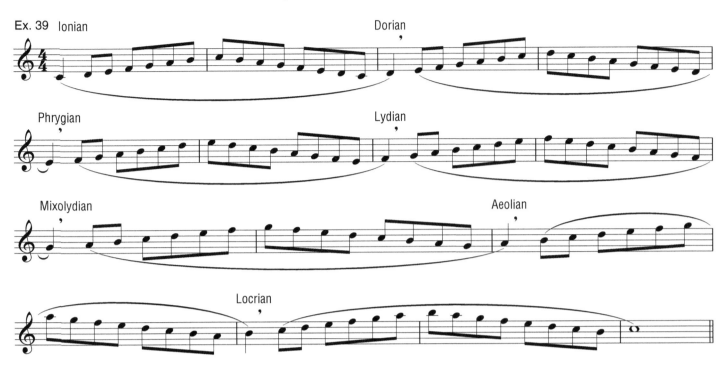

Ex. 39 Ionian   Dorian

Phrygian   Lydian

Mixolydian   Aeolian

Locrian

MORE ABOUT MODES

If you examine the previous chart closely, you will notice that the whole step/half-step intervals change from mode to mode. This provides you with yet another way to understand and analyze modes. For example, rather than seeing D Dorian and thinking of it as the second mode of C major, you could analyze D Dorian as a D major scale with flatted 3rd and flatted 7th degrees. To the right are the scale formulas necessary to generate each of the seven modes using this method.

This way of thinking of modes may allow you to hear and understand better the sounds that various modes produce. For example, in situations where one chord, Dm7, is played for a long time, you might improvise using D Dorian, D Phrygian, or D Aeolian.

IONIAN: 1–2–3–4–5–6–7

DORIAN: 1–2–♭3–4–5–6–♭7

PHRYGIAN: 1–♭2–♭3–4–5–♭6–♭7

LYDIAN: 1–2–3–♯4–5–6–7

MIXOLYDIAN: 1–2–3–4–5–6–♭7

AEOLIAN: 1–2–♭3–4–5–♭6–♭7

LOCRIAN: 1–♭2–♭3–4–♭5–♭6–♭7

THE HARMONIC MINOR SCALE

The *harmonic minor scale* has been used for centuries in many different contexts. Its unique construction produces many interesting sounds and makes it a frequent and compelling choice among jazz musicians.

Construction

The step pattern for the harmonic minor scale is whole–half–whole–whole–half–whole+half–half. To build a C harmonic minor scale, start with the note C and follow the pattern accordingly.

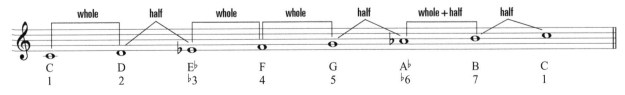

whole   half   whole   whole   half   whole + half   half

C   D   E♭   F   G   A♭   B   C
1   2   ♭3   4   5   ♭6   7   1

The harmonic minor scale can also be thought of as a major scale with flatted 3rd and 6th degrees, or a natural minor scale with a raised 7th degree.

Chords

The seventh chords built on the C harmonic minor scale are:

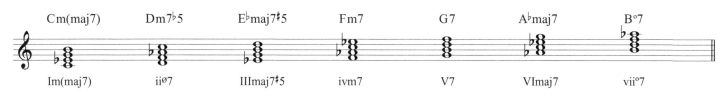

Modes

In jazz music, the modes of the harmonic minor scale—especially the second, fifth, and seventh—are used very often. To become familiar with the harmonic-minor modes, practice them as shown in Exercise 40.

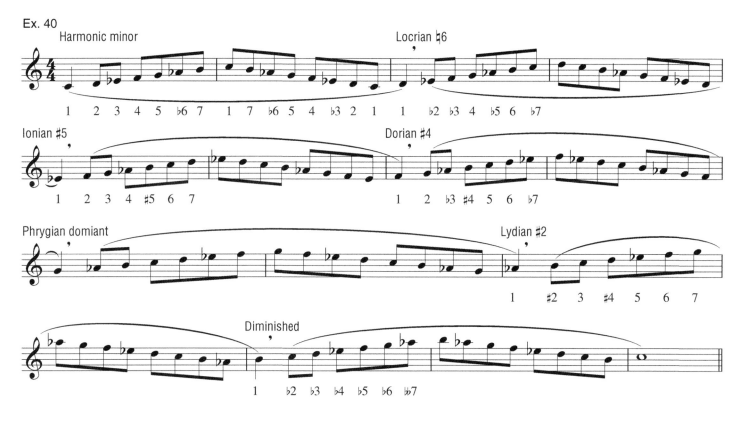

THE MELODIC MINOR SCALE

The *melodic minor scale* is commonly referred to as the "jazz minor scale." Its distinctive character generates many familiar jazz sounds. In fact, the melodic minor scale is used by jazz musicians as frequently as the major scale.

Construction

The step pattern for the melodic minor scale is whole–half–whole–whole–whole–whole–half. To build a C melodic minor scale, start with the note C and follow the pattern accordingly:

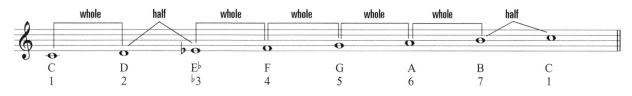

The melodic minor scale can also be thought of as a major scale with a flatted 3rd degree, or a natural minor scale with raised 6th and 7th degrees.

Chords

The seventh chords built on the C melodic minor scale are:

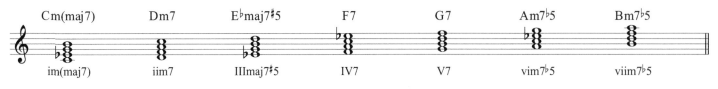

Cm(maj7)	Dm7	E♭maj7♯5	F7	G7	Am7♭5	Bm7♭5
im(maj7)	iim7	IIImaj7♯5	IV7	V7	vim7♭5	viim7♭5

Modes

In jazz music, the modes of the melodic minor scale—especially the fourth, sixth, and seventh—are used very often. Practice the modes of the melodic minor scale in Exercise 41.

Ex. 41

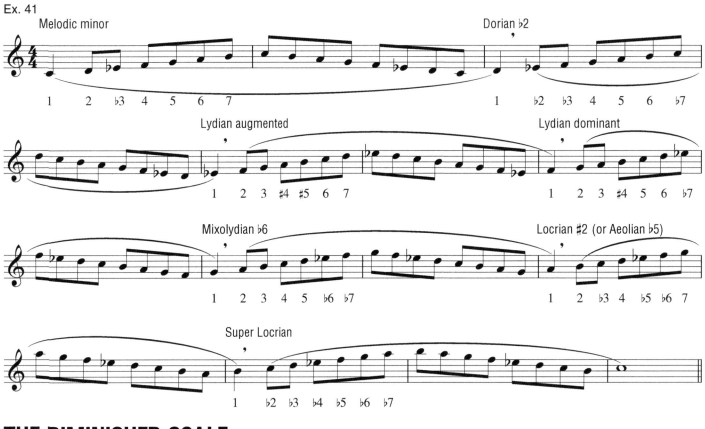

THE DIMINISHED SCALE

The *diminished scale* (also called the *octatonic scale*) is a symmetrical scale built from alternating whole steps and half steps. This alternating pattern results in two variations: the *half-whole* and *whole-half*.

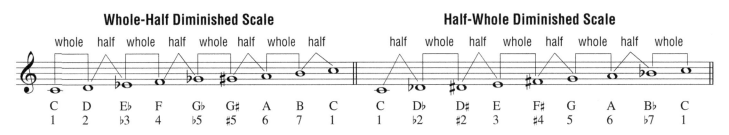

Notice that these scales repeat themselves every time they are played a minor 3rd higher. As a result, the C diminished scale contains the same notes as the E♭ (D♯), G♭ (F♯), and A diminished scales.

The half-whole diminished scale is used over dominant seventh chords that have a V–I relationship. Play the scale up and down through one octave to become familiar with it. Then try two octaves. Keep playing until you've memorized the scale. Now start on E♭, playing the same scale up and down. Continue the exercise by starting on F♯, then on A. Each time you play the scale, think of the chords that share the scale tones (i.e., C7, E♭7, F♯7, A7). Repeat in every key.

Exercises 42–45 demonstrate short patterns using the half-whole diminished scale.

Ex. 42 C7, C7♭9, or C7♯9

Ex. 43 C7, C7♭9, or C7♯9

Ex. 44 C7, C7♭9, or C7♯9

Ex. 45 C7, C7♭9, or C7♯9

The whole-half diminished scale is used over diminished chords. Play the scale up and down one octave to become familiar with it. Then try two octaves. Keep playing until you've memorized the scale. Now start on E♭, playing the same scale up and down. Continue the exercise by starting on F♯, then on A. Each time you play the scale, think of the chords that share the scale tones (i.e., Cdim7, E♭dim7, F♯dim7, Adim7). Repeat in every key.

Short patterns based on the whole-half diminished scale are shown in Exercises 46–48.

Ex. 46 C°7, E♭°7, F♯°7, or A°7

Ex. 47 C°7, E♭°7, F♯°7, or A°7

Ex. 48 C°7, E♭°7, F♯°7, or A°7

THE WHOLE-TONE SCALE

The *whole-tone scale* is a symmetrical scale built entirely of whole steps, or whole tones.

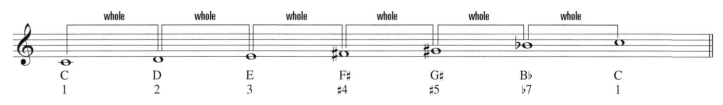

	whole	whole	whole	whole	whole	whole
C	D	E	F♯	G♯	B♭	C
1	2	3	♯4	♯5	♭7	1

Notice that this scale repeats itself every time it is played a whole step higher. As a result, the C whole-tone scale contains the same notes as the D, E, F♯ (G♭), G♯ (A♭), and A♯ (B♭) whole-tone scales. Likewise, the C♯ (D♭) whole-tone scale contains the same notes as the D♯ (E♭), F, G, A, and B whole-tone scales.

The whole-tone scale works well over augmented triads and dominant seventh chords with any combination of raised or lowered fifths and major ninths. All of the intervals are major 2nds (whole tones), providing a very exotic sound. Every note in the whole-tone scale works well over the chords shown, with the augmented 5th giving the scale its unique sound.

Exercises 49–55 contain short patterns employing the whole-tone scale.

IMPROVISING OVER DOMINANT CHORDS

There are seven different scales that work well over dominant chords. Following is an explanation of when and how each scale is used, along with common licks to help illustrate the resulting sounds and develop your vocabulary. The next several examples (Tracks 36–42) all use scales starting with G.

Mixolydian (1-2-3-4-5-6-♭7)

The *Mixolydian* mode is best suited for playing over unaltered dominant chords (e.g., 7th, 9th, 11th, 13th). It effectively complements these chords in both *cadential*, or functioning, harmonic progressions (such as a resolving V–I progression) and *non-cadential*, or non-functioning, harmonic progressions (such as a non-resolving V–IV progression).

TRACK 36

Phrygian Dominant (1-♭2-3-4-5-♭6-♭7)

Phrygian dominant, the fifth mode of harmonic minor, is best suited for playing over 7♭9, 7♯9, or 7♭9♯9 chords. It also works well over unaltered dominant chords. The scale is usually used in cadential harmonic progressions that resolve to either a im7 or Imaj7 chord.

TRACK 37

Lydian Dominant (1-2-3-♯4-5-6-♭7)

The *Lydian dominant* scale (a.k.a. Mixolydian ♯4) is best suited for playing over 7♯11, or 7♭5, chords. It also works well over unaltered dominant chords. The scale is usually used in non-cadential harmonic progressions.

TRACK 38

Super Locrian (1-♭2-♭3-♭4-♭5-♭6-♭7)

The *super Locrian* scale (a.k.a. the altered scale) is best suited for playing over altered dominant chords (e.g., 7♯9, 7♯5, 7♭9, 7♭5, 7♯9/♯5, 7♭9/♭5, 7♯9/♭5, 7♭9/♯5). Since the alterations create so much dissonance, the scale is almost always used in cadential, or resolving, harmonic progressions.

TRACK 39

Dominant Diminished (1-♭2-♯2-3-♯4-5-6-♭7)

The *dominant diminished* scale (a.k.a. half-whole diminished) is best suited for playing over chords with ♭5, ♭9, and ♯9 alterations. It also works well over unaltered dominant chords. The scale is usually used in cadential harmonic progressions.

TRACK 40

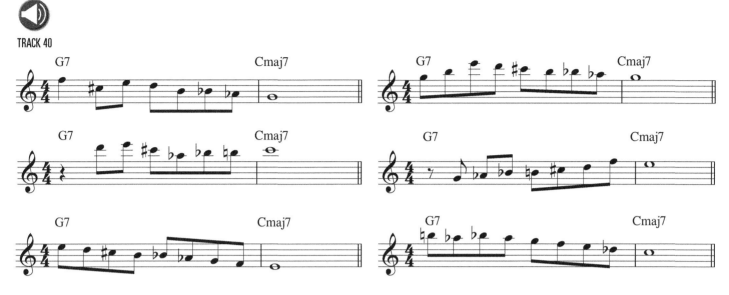

Whole-Tone (1-2-3-♯4-♯5-♭7)

The *whole-tone* scale is best suited for playing over 7♯5 chords, but it also works well over unaltered dominant chords. The scale can be used in both cadential and non-cadential harmonic progressions.

TRACK 41

Mixolydian ♭6 (1-2-3-4-5-♭6-♭7)

Mixolydian ♭6, the fifth mode of melodic minor, is best suited for playing over 7♯5 and 9♯5 chords (note that the ninth should not be altered). It also works well over unaltered dominant chords. The scale can be used in either cadential or non-cadential harmonic progressions.

TRACK 42

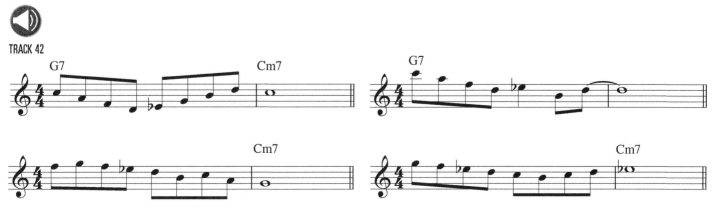

IMPROVISING OVER MAJOR CHORDS

There are three different scales that work well over major chords. Following is an explanation of when and how each scale is used, along with common licks to help illustrate the resulting sounds and develop your vocabulary.

Ionian (1-2-3-4-5-6-7)

The *Ionian* mode, (a.k.a.) the major scale, is best suited for playing over maj7, maj9, and maj13 chords. Note that the scale's 4th degree is often avoided—that is, it is sometimes played but rarely emphasized.

TRACK 43

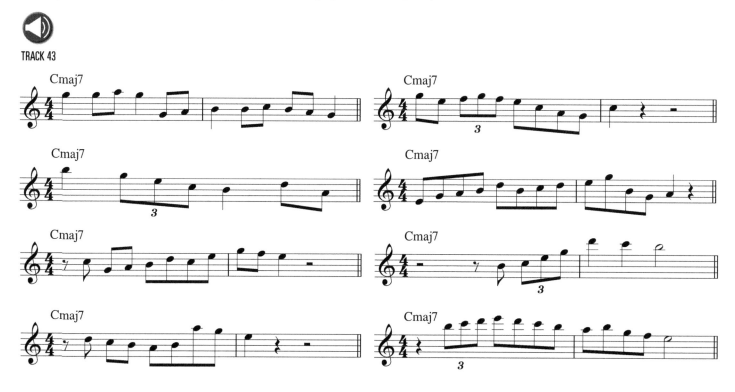

Lydian (1-2-3-♯4-5-6-7)

The *Lydian* mode is best suited for playing over maj7♯11 chords, but it also works well over maj7, maj9, and maj13 chords.

TRACK 44

Lydian ♯2 (1-♯2-3-♯4-5-6-7)

The *Lydian ♯2* scale, the sixth mode of harmonic minor, is best suited for playing over maj7♯11 chords, but it also works well over maj7, maj9, and maj13 chords.

TRACK 45

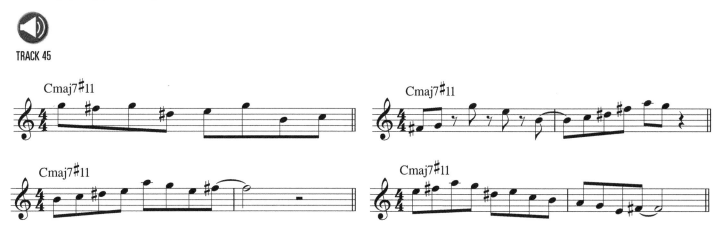

IMPROVISING OVER MINOR CHORDS

There are seven different scales that can be played over minor chords. Two of these scales—Dorian ♯4 and Dorian ♭2—are used less frequently than the others and are therefore omitted from this lesson. Following is an explanation of when and how each scale is used, along with common licks as illustrated.

Dorian (1-2-♭3-4-5-6-♭7)

The *Dorian* mode is best suited for playing over m6, m7, m9, and m11 chords. It is typically employed over minor chords functioning as ii chords, but also effectively complements im7 chords.

TRACK 46

Harmonic Minor (1-2-♭3-4-5-♭6-7)

The *harmonic minor* scale is generally the first choice for improvising over m(maj7), m7, m9, and m11 chords when they are functioning as tonic i chords. Its design, does not, however, effectively complement m6 chords.

TRACK 47

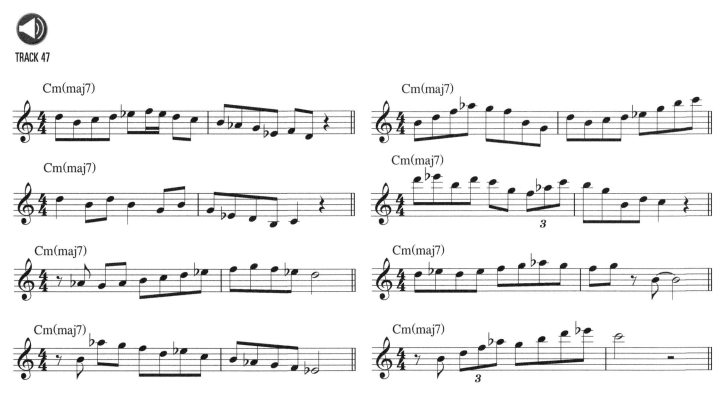

Melodic Minor (1-2-♭3-4-5-6-7)

The *melodic minor* scale works best over m(maj7) and m6 chords when they are functioning as tonic i chords, but it also works well over m7, m9, and m11 chords.

TRACK 48

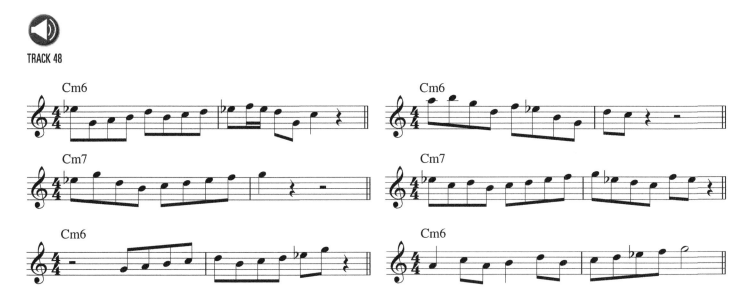

Aeolian (1-2-♭3-4-5-♭6-♭7)

The *Aeolian* mode can be used over any m7, m9, or m11 chord. It is suitable over these chords when they are functioning as vi chords. The scale should be avoided when playing over m6 chords.

TRACK 49

Phrygian (1-♭2-♭3-4-5-♭6-♭7)

The *Phrygian* mode is best suited for playing over m7 and m11 chords. However, it should not be used over m6 or m9 chords.

TRACK 50

IMPROVISING OVER MINOR 7♭5 CHORDS

There are three main scales that can be played over m7♭5 chords. Once again, here are explanations and demonstrations of when and how each scale is used. The examples in the section use scales starting on D.

Locrian ♮6 (1-♭2-♭3-4-♭5-6-♭7)

Locrian ♮6, the sixth mode of harmonic minor, is most often used over a m7♭5 chord within a progression approaching the V chord (e.g., Dm7♭5–G7♭9–Cm7 or Dm7♭5–G7–Cmaj7).

TRACK 51

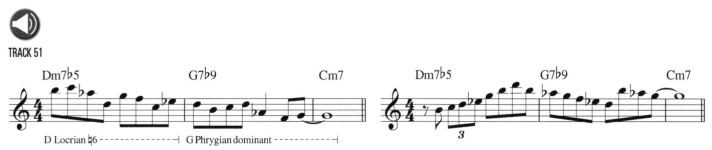

Locrian #2 (1-2-♭3-4-♭5-♭6-♭7)

Locrian #2, a mode of melodic minor, is also most often used over a m7♭5 chord within a progression approaching a V chord.

TRACK 52

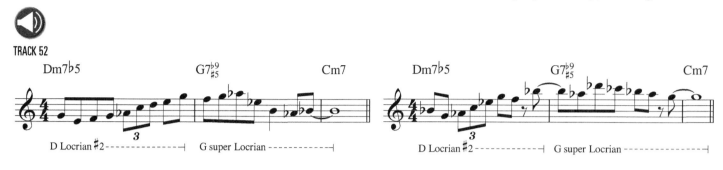

Locrian (1-♭2-♭3-4-♭5-♭6-♭7)

The *Locrian* mode is best suited for playing over a m7♭5 chord that is functioning as a vii chord. It can also be used over a m7♭5 chord that is played for a long time.

TRACK 53

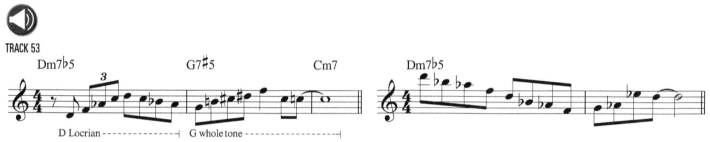

IMPROVISING OVER DIMINISHED SEVENTH CHORDS

There are two different scales that can be played over diminished seventh chords. The *diminished mode* (vii of harmonic minor) is best suited over dim7 chords that resolve up a half step. The *whole-half diminished scale* works well over dim7 chords that resolve either up or down.

Diminished Mode (1-♭2-♭3-♭4-♭5-♭6-♭♭7)

TRACK 54

Whole-Half Diminished Scale (1-2-♭3-4-♭5-♯5-6-7)

TRACK 55

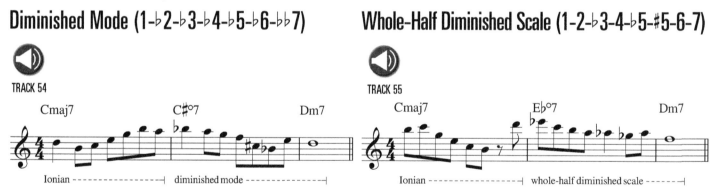

IMPROVISING OVER MAJOR 7♯5 CHORDS

There are two different scales that can be played over maj7♯5 chords: *Ionian ♯5* and *Lydian augmented* (the III modes of harmonic minor and melodic minor, respectively).

Ionian ♯5 (1-2-3-4-♯5-6-7)

TRACK 56

Lydian Augmented (1-2-3-♯4-♯5-6-7)

TRACK 57

PENTATONIC SCALES

The *pentatonic scale* is a five-note scale using degrees 1–2–3–5–6 of a major scale; the 4th and 7th degrees are omitted, thus eliminating the half steps. The major and minor pentatonic belong to the same modal family. For instance, the G minor pentatonic contains the same notes as the B♭ major pentatonic. The absence of notes that need to be resolved (the 4th and 7th degrees) gives the pentatonic scale its characteristic open sound. John Coltrane led the use of pentatonic scales in jazz during the '60s.

G Major Pentatonic

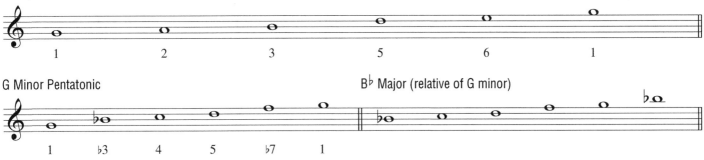

G Minor Pentatonic   B♭ Major (relative of G minor)

Pentatonics Over Dominant Chords

The pentatonic scale based on the root of the dominant seventh is best suited to unaltered dominant seventh chords.

TRACK 58

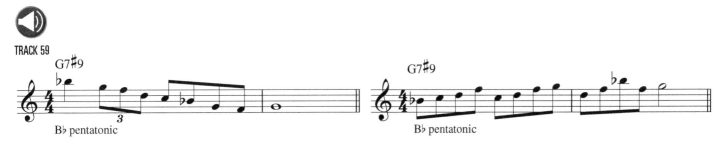

The major pentatonic scale a minor 3rd above the root is best suited for a dominant ♯9 chord.

TRACK 59

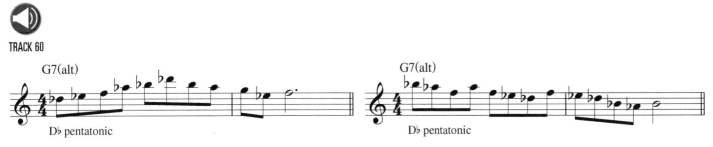

For altered chords, the major pentatonic a tritone away from the root is the best choice.

TRACK 60

For a dominant 7♯9♭13, use the major pentatonic built off of the ♭13.

TRACK 61

The major pentatonic a whole step below the root is best suited for sus4 chords.

TRACK 62

Pentatonics Over Major Chords

When improvising over major chords, you have three options: the major pentatonic built off the root, the major pentatonic built off the fifth (which provides more color notes, like the seventh and ninth), or the major pentatonic built off of the ninth (which is best suited to maj7#11 chords).

TRACK 63

Pentatonics Over Minor Chords

There are three pentatonic scales that work well over minor chords: the minor pentatonic off the root, the minor pentatonic off the fifth, and the minor pentatonic off the ninth.

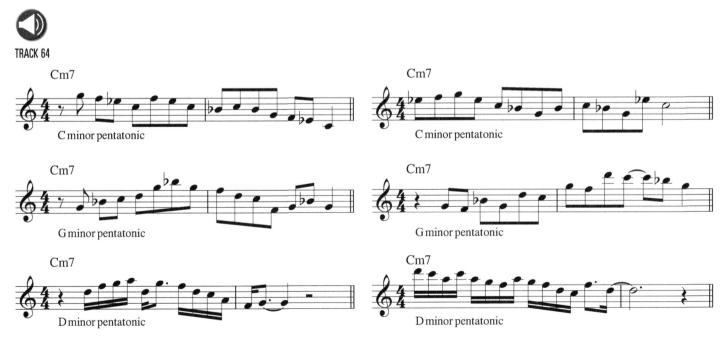

TRACK 64

Pentatonics Over ii–V–I Progressions

The major pentatonic off the 5th scale degree is best suited to a ii–V–I progression if the V chord is not altered, as Track 65 demonstrates.

TRACK 65

For more harmonic variety, use the D minor pentatonic for the ii chord, the major pentatonic a tritone away from the root for the altered V chord, and the major pentatonic off the root for the I chord.

TRACK 66

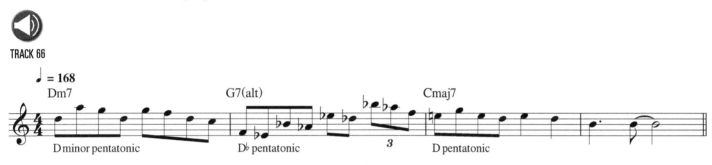

Track 67 adds further wrinkles by using the minor pentatonics built off the root and fifth of the ii chord, the major pentatonic a tritone away from the root for the V chord, and the major pentatonic off the ninth for the I chord.

TRACK 67

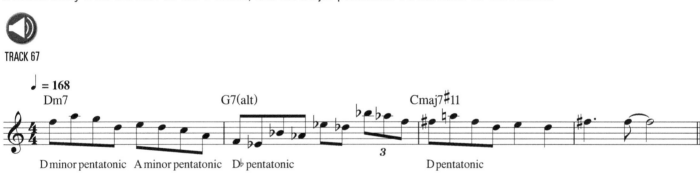

ETUDES AND EXERCISES

This section contains etudes and exercises based on scales and chords common in jazz playing. Incorporating these exercises into your daily practice routine will result in improved technique and the ability to color the harmonic materials of jazz. For more patterns and exercises, check out *Amazing Phrasing*, published by Hal Leonard.

SPEED DRILLS

First is a major-scale drill designed to increase finger speed. Practice it slowly with a metronome. Gradually increase the setting of the metronome as your dexterity improves. Learn the exercise in every key.

Ex. 56

The next exercise provides a framework for practicing a variety of scales used in jazz. The scales are whole-tone, Lydian, major, minor, whole-half diminished, and half-whole diminished. Again, practice with a metronome, gradually increasing the tempo. Strive for evenness, and learn the pattern in every key.

Ex. 57

MELODIC 4THS

Because the chords of jazz are mainly built from 3rds, 3rds tend to figure prominently in improvised melodic lines. But we needn't limit ourselves to 3rds. Practicing exercises in 4ths can enrich the melodic vocabulary that you can draw upon in your solos.

Exercise 58 plays a major scale in 4ths. Practice it in every key.

Ex. 58

Exercise 59 alternates ascending and descending perfect 4ths over the entire range of the saxophone.

Ex. 59

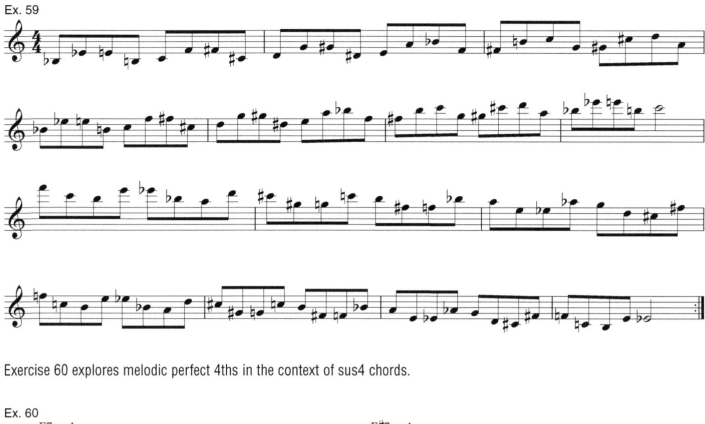

Exercise 60 explores melodic perfect 4ths in the context of sus4 chords.

Ex. 60

BEBOP MIXOLYDIAN SCALE

The *bebop Mixolydian scale*—a scale with an added half step between the root and the lowered 7th—was used by improvisers of the 1940s bebop era.

This scale facilitates bebop's quick tempos, as exemplified in Exercise 61. The scale should be mastered in all keys to help you gain facility in using this as an improvisational tool.

Ex. 61

Exercise 62 shows the C bebop Mixolydian scale in use over a ii–V–I progression in F major.

Track 68 is a three-chorus etude based on the composition "Tune-up." The first chorus features a common lick derived from the bebop Mixolydian scale, which is then transposed through the appropriate keys of the song. The second chorus uses the scale descending and ascending, forming a symmetrical phrase. Measures 16 and 32 act as *turnarounds*, transitional phrases that link one chorus to the next. The third chorus introduces yet another lick utilizing the bebop Mixolydian scale.

TRACK 68

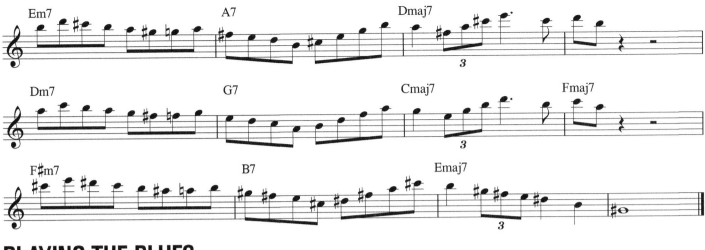

PLAYING THE BLUES

The blues is a twelve-bar format used as the basis of many jazz songs. Some claim one's ability to play the blues really demonstrates one's overall musicianship.

Blues Scale

The *blues scale* is a six-note scale comprised of 1–♭3–4–♭5–5–♭7. The ♭3 and ♭5 give it its characteristic bluesy sound.

G blues scale

The beauty of this is that you can use one scale for the entire twelve-bar blues. Practice soloing using the blues scale along with the accompaniment on Track 69. Remember to vary the rhythms and lengths of phrases. Use the entire range of your saxophone and strive for lines that have contour to them. This will create more excitement and give your solo a sense of motion. Staying in a narrow range for too long will cause you to lose direction. Pay close attention to how you resolve the ♭5 and avoid large interval skips with that note. It wants to resolve by half step, either up to the 5th or down to the 4th.

Now play the head and written solo choruses to "To Be or B♭." The third and fourth choruses demonstrate a guide-tone line (chorus numbers are indicated by boxed numerals). A *guide-tone line* is based on the third or seventh of each chord, and weaves its way through the progression by moving in half or whole steps. Learning where the resolutions are when moving from chord to chord will enhance your lines and train your ear. The fifth and sixth choruses are designed to help you get beyond the blues scale and get inside the chords.

TO BE OR B♭

TRACK 69

52

TRITONE SUBSTITUTION

Jazz musicians frequently substitute one chord for another to create more interesting harmonies. One of the most common substitution techniques is called *tritone substitution*. Here the concept is to replace a chord with the dominant chord three whole steps (i.e., a tritone) away. This produces harmonic tension, yet allows smooth voice leading from chord to chord.

Why does this work? Well, let's look at the individual notes of each chord. A7 contains the notes A–C♯–E–G. E♭7 contains the notes E♭–G–B♭–D♭(C♯). Thus the thirds and sevenths of both chords are the same.

The soloist can plug in the substitutions whether the rhythm section plays them or not. An experienced rhythm section will pick up on what you're doing and start playing the substitutions with you. The etude in Track 70 uses only chord tones. The substitutions are in parentheses. The rhythm section does not play the substitutions in the first half of the etude, so you can hear the effect of the soloist playing substitutions over the original chords. Beginning at letter B, the rhythm section plays the substitutions with the soloist.

TRACK 70

IMPROVISATION TIP

The tritone substitution works best when the two chords (i.e., the chord being substituted for, and the chord it resolves to) are a 5th apart. When playing substitutions, keep it simple: chord tones work best.

MELODIC EMBELLISHMENTS

Passing Tones

Just as English grammar uses labels such as "conjunction," "preposition," and "pronoun" to indicate parts of speech or other functional classifications, music has its own terminology to identify compositional and improvisational techniques. By definition, *passing tones* are not part of the song's harmony, but serve to connect two notes that are. For example, if you played the notes C–C#–D over a Cmaj13 chord, C# would be considered a passing tone. The lick below is a typical phrase in the jazz lexicon that uses passing tones chromatically. Notice that the passing tones themselves, which are circled, fall on upbeats. In general, this is the best spot to weave them into the fabric of your lines.

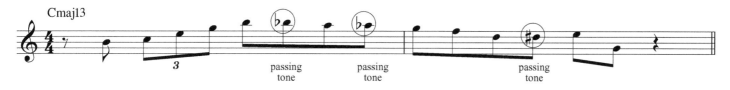

When passing tones are positioned chromatically, as in the phrase above, they are sometimes referred to as "chromatic passing tones." However, the term *chromaticism* is a much broader expression that describes the use of any notes outside the song's key—not necessarily between two chord tones.

Neighbor Tones and Surround Tones

While we're on the subject, you should also become familiar with two more labels: neighbor tones and surround tones. A *neighbor tone* is a nonharmonic note on the weak beat that moves a half or whole step above or below another note and then returns to that note. *Surround tones* are notes that combine to circle above and below a target note. They anticipate the resolution of the third note, thereby establishing the color and harmony of the ensuing chord. Check out the lick below for a sample of neighbor tones and surround tones in action.

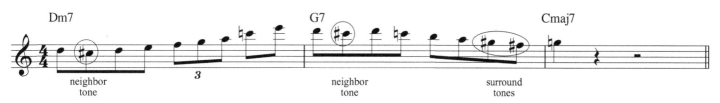

Exercise 63, based on the major scale, demonstrates a use of neighbor tones. Learn it in every key.

Exercise 64 decorates an arpeggio exercise with neighbor tones.

Ex. 64

Exercise 65 demonstrates neighbor and passing tones in the circle of 5ths.

Exercise 66 explores surround tones in strings of ascending 4ths.

Ex. 66

Exercises 67–74 demonstrate various melodic embellishments in iim7–V7–Imaj7 progressions. Run each of these patterns through the changing harmonies of Track 24.

PLAYING FROM A FAKE BOOK

A *fake book* is a collection of lead sheets, usually presenting the tunes with just the melody and chord symbols. The best and most accurate fake books are the volumes of *The Real Book*, published by Hal Leonard.

The melody on a lead sheet is generally written within the staff for easy reading. This is a simplified, basic guideline to the song. Re-phrasing the melody is up to your interpretation. If you've heard a recording of the song, you'll have an idea of what to do; if not, you'll just have to rely on your musical instincts. A good general rule is to try phrasing like a singer. (Remember, the tenor sax is a B♭ instrument, so if you're reading from a concert-pitch (C) lead sheet you'll need to transpose up a whole step.)

The following is a lead sheet of the standard "I Remember You," showing how it would appear in a "C Instruments" fake book.

I REMEMBER YOU

Theme from the Paramount Picture THE FLEET'S IN

Exercise 75 demonstrates how a tenor saxophonist might interpret the melody. It also shows the chart transposed up a step to the key of G to accomodate the B♭ tenor sax. (Note: if a tenor sax player read from a "B♭ Instruments" fake book, no transposition would be necessary.)

I REMEMBER YOU

Ex. 75

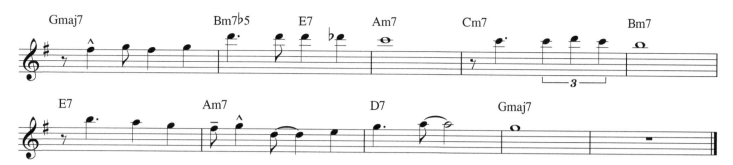

You will need to memorize songs to develop a repertoire. When learning a new melody, first play through it a few times. As you get comfortable with it, break down the phrases. If it is a standard AABA thirty-two-measure format, you will notice that the A sections are essentially the same (sometimes there are slight differences at the final cadences—measures 7–8). That leaves only the eight measures in the bridge to memorize. This is the case with "Satin Doll," shown below. Here the bridge moves up a 4th to the key of A minor, a common harmonic device. The melody descends down the scale off of the 5th. The second four measures of the bridge repeat the same thing a whole step higher.

After you've learned the melody, you need to learn the chord changes. Grouping the chords together in key centers will help you organize the changes. In the A sections, you have two measures in the key of D major, up a whole step to E major for two measures, then A for one measure, down a half step to A♭ for one measure, then two measures back in the key of E minor. The bridge moves up a 4th to the key of G major with a ii–V–I over four measures followed by a ii–V–I a whole step higher in the key of A major. An A7 in measure 8 returns us to the key of E minor. By using this grouping technique, you will have fewer chords to memorize—and the tonal centers will be more apparent. Learning the changes by designating numbers (i.e., ii, V, etc.) will be helpful if you ever have to transpose a song to another key.

To practice the song, start by playing the melody. Next, arpeggiate the harmonies in root position; then begin voice leading the chords, gradually working toward being able to play the chords in any position and any direction.

SATIN DOLL
from SOPHISTICATED LADIES

It is a common practice in jazz to write a new melody over an existing set of chord changes. Knowing some examples will help expand your repertoire. Some heads will follow the original changes closely, while others might combine the chords to two different songs (like the A section of "Honeysuckle Rose" and the B section of "I've Got Rhythm"). The following is a short list of tunes and the models on which they are based.

Tune	Model
Al-Leu-Cha	Honeysuckle Rose
Countdown	Tune-up
Dig	Sweet Georgia Brown
Donna Lee	Back Home in Indiana
Evidence	Just You, Just Me
Groovin' High	Whispering
Half Nelson	Lady Bird
Prince Albert	All the Things You Are
In Walked Bud	Blue Skies
Ko-Ko	Cherokee
Warming Up a Riff	Cherokee
Anthropology	I've Got Rhythm
Meet the Flintstones	I've Got Rhythm
Oleo	I've Got Rhythm
Rhythm-a-ning	I've Got Rhythm

MUST-KNOW STANDARDS

Straight-ahead Swing	Ballad	Waltz	Bossa Nova
1. All the Things You Are	1. Body and Soul	1. Alice in Wonderland	1. Black Orpheus
2. Autumn Leaves	2. Here's That Rainy Day	2. All Blues	2. Blue Bossa
3. The Days of Wine and Roses	3. In a Sentimental Mood	3. Bluesette	3. The Girl from Ipanema
4. A Foggy Day	4. Misty	4. Falling in Love with Love	4. How Insensitive
5. Have You Met Miss Jones?	5. My Foolish Heart	5. Fly Me to the Moon	5. Redcorda-me
6. Just Friends	6. My Funny Valentine	6. Footprints	6. The Shadow of Your Smile
7. My Romance	7. My One and Only Love	7. My Favorite Things	7. Song for My Father
8. Satin Doll	8. 'Round Midnight	8. Someday My Prince Will Come	8. So Nice (Summer Samba)
9. Stella by Starlight	9. When I Fall in Love	9. Tenderly	9. Watch What Happens
10. There Will Never Be Another You	10. When Sunny Gets Blue	10. Windows	10. Wave

LICK SUBSTITUTION

Nearly every phrase in the jazz vocabulary can be employed in multiple contexts. Below are several variations of one of Charlie Parker's favorite phrases. With careful attention to resolution and slight variations in notes and rhythm, he is able to use this lick in many different ways.

LICK SUBSTITUTION

Use the following chart as a guide to lick substitution.

Play any **Dmaj7** idea over	Play any **Dm7** idea over	Play any **G7** idea over
Am7	Bm7♭5	Dm7
D13	C#7 $^{♭9}_{#5}$	Bm7♭5
F#m7♭5	G9	C#7 $^{♭9}_{#5}$
Cmaj7	G11	
D7sus4	G13	
B7($^{♭9}_{♭5}$)		
B7($^{♯9}_{#5}$)		
Fmaj#11		

SOLOING STYLES

The saxophone in jazz has a rich and varied history. It is important to be familiar with as many different styles as possible. Each student should know the horn's legacy.

This section demonstrates many diverse styles and approaches to improvisation, along with acquainting the student with the main practitioners of each style.

EARLY SWING

Coleman Hawkins, Lester Young, and Ben Webster were the most notable saxophone pioneers who cultivated jazz improvisation in the 1920s and 1930s. Typical solos from the era featured arpeggios, blues inflections, few altered notes, fluid rhythmic phrasing, and a propensity to stay close to the song's melody.

INDIANA (BACK HOME AGAIN IN INDIANA)

TRACK 71

Words by BALLARD MACDONALD
Music by JAMES F. HANLEY
Copyright © 2009 by HAL LEONARD CORPORATION
International Copyright Secured   All Rights Reserved

MAINSTREAM JAZZ

Stan Getz, Dexter Gordon, and Zoot Sims are often associated with mainstream or "straight-ahead" jazz. Their improvisation styles are characterized by melodic scale-like lines, a keen harmonic sense, passing tones, and nice swinging phrasing.

"Autumn Leaves" is a classic mid-tempo jazz standard. Lay back on the eighth notes to help capture the requisite swing feel.

AUTUMN LEAVES

TRACK 72

English lyric by JOHNNY MERCER
French lyric by JACQUES PREVERT
Music by JOSEPH KOSMA

BOSSA NOVA

It's also important to develop your improvisational skills in a Latin setting. Most licks and phrases can be assimilated into the style's even-eighth-note feel; however, it helps to emphasize rhythmic syncopation.

MEDITATION (MEDITAÇÃO)

TRACK 73

Music by ANTONIO CARLOS JOBIM
Original Words by NEWTON MENDONCA
English Words by NORMAN GIMBEL

BALLAD

Improvising on ballads can be challenging. The chord changes move slowly, but the feel and phrasing require rhythmic command and lots of patience. Some players prefer to feel slower tempos in double time. Other players elect to balance simple phrases played "in time" with long runs played *rubato*, or "out of time."

EASY LIVING
Theme from the Paramount Picture *EASY LIVING*

TRACK 74

Words and Music by LEO ROBIN and RALPH RAINGER
Copyright © 1937 Sony/ATV Music Publishing LLC
Copyright Renewed
All Rights Administered by Sony/ATV Music Publishing LLC, 8 Music Square West, Nashville, TN 37203
International Copyright Secured   All Rights Reserved

BEBOP

Bebop allowed jazz improvisers to showcase their formidable technique and adventurous harmonic sense. Bop saxophone stylists such as Charlie Parker, Sonny Stitt, Johnny Griffin, and James Moody exhibited fleet phrases full of dazzling melodic invention and lots of altered notes.

BE-BOP

TRACK 75

BLUES

The twelve-bar blues progression is used frequently in all genres of jazz, but it is especially prevalent in bebop. Some bebop blues tunes such as "Blues for Alice" contain extra chord changes. Others, such as "Now's the Time," "Straight, No Chaser," and "Tenor Madness," follow the more conventional form found on Track 76.

BLUES IN C

TRACK 76

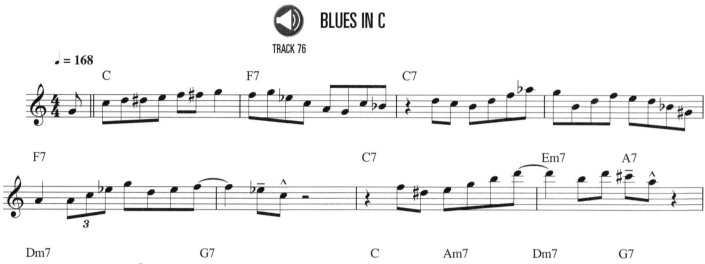

RHYTHM CHANGES

Many bebop tunes such as "Oleo" and "Moose the Mooche" are based on the chord changes of the Gershwin classic "I Got Rhythm." These tunes follow a thirty-two-measure AABA form. The A sections make use of an eight-bar tonic-based progression. In the bridge, the song moves up a major 3rd, using the cycle of 5ths to work its way back to the tonic.

RHYTHM CHANGES IN C

POST-BOP BOSSA NOVA

The mid 1950s ushered in a harder-driving style of improvisation, exemplified by tenor saxophonists such as John Coltrane, Sonny Rollins, Hank Mobley, and Joe Henderson. "Song for My Father" is just one of the bossa novas popularized in the post-bop era.

SONG FOR MY FATHER

TRACK 78

× = add right hand

Words and Music by HORACE SILVER
© 1964, 1966, 1969, 1987 by Ecaroh Music, Inc.
Copyright Renewed 1992
International Copyright Secured   All Rights Reserved

MODAL JAZZ

In the 1960s, musicians began composing songs with static chords and repeated vamps rather than moving changes. This simpler, more atmospheric framework became known as *modal jazz*—so named because improvisers experimented with playing several related scales or modes over a single chord. The following solo is based on the Dorian mode.

SO WHAT

TRACK 79

By MILES DAVIS
Copyright © 1959 JAZZ HORN MUSIC CORP.
Copyright Renewed
All Rights Controlled and Administered by SONGS OF UNIVERSAL, INC.
All Rights Reserved   Used by Permission

DOMINANT-SEVENTH-BASED TUNE

"Doxy" relies heavily on dominant seventh chords, including the altered A7#9. "Sweet Georgia Brown," "Sister Sadie," "The Preacher," and "Well You Needn't" are other songs using dominant seventh chords almost exclusively.

DOXY
TRACK 80

By SONNY ROLLINS
Copyright © 1963 Prestige Music
Copyright Renewed
International Copyright Secured   All Rights Reserved

ALTERED CHORDS

An important step in being able to create interesting lines in your solos is understanding how to alter a song's chords. Altering the extensions of chords (usually the fifth, ninth, eleventh, or thirteenth) will add tension and dissonance. The following solo is based on the chords to "Stella by Starlight." Notice how the altered chords add harmonic interest and aid in smooth voice leading from chord to chord.

TWILIGHT TIME

TRACK 81

MINOR BLUES

Altered chords appear also in this minor blues. "Equinox," "Chitlins con Carne," and "Mr. P.C." are other minor blues from the post-bop era.

D MINOR BLUES

TRACK 82

FUNK JAZZ

Creating a solo over one chord sounds simple, but can prove to be quite challenging. One way to approach playing over a static harmony is to create tension and release by moving in and out of other tonal centers. This can be accomplished by taking a four-note grouping and sequencing through other keys before returning to the original key. Michael Brecker, Bob Mintzer, Chris Potter, and Bob Berg are all masters of this.

IN AND OUT

TRACK 83

× = add right hand

SLASH CHORDS

Slash chords are chords with a bass tone other than the root of the chord. The letter on the left-hand side of the slash is the chord and the letter on the right-hand side is the bass note. The first chord of "Maiden Voyage" is Bm (B–D–F♯) over E. If you consider E the root, this will give you the fifth, seventh, and ninth of an E chord. Notice there is no third. Without the third, you don't know if the chord is major or minor, which creates an ambiguous, open sound. Using wider intervals (putting some "air" between the notes) will contribute to the unique nature of these chords.

MAIDEN VOYAGE

TRACK 84

3/4 METER

"Footprints," composed by saxophonist Wayne Shorter, is a bit of an oddity in the jazz-standard repertoire. It is a twenty-four-measure minor blues in 3/4 time.

FOOTPRINTS

TRACK 85

SOUL JAZZ

Soul jazz is a sub-genre from the post-bop era that emphasizes R&B rhythms and blues-inflected improvisations. Saxophonists like Stanley Turrentine, Willis Jackson, and David "Fathead" Newman are notable exponents of this style. A few popular songs include "Mercy, Mercy, Mercy," "Hard Times," and "Road Song."

SOUL BENEFACTOR

TRACK 86

CONTEMPORARY

This solo incorporates contemporary harmonic devices like chromaticism, altered tones, and playing a half step above the chords.

CHI CHI

TRACK 87

HAL•LEONARD® SAXOPHONE PLAY-ALONG

The Saxophone Play-Along Series will help you play your favorite songs quickly and easily. Just follow the music, listen to the audio to hear how the saxophone should sound, and then play along using the separate backing tracks. Each song is printed twice in the book: once for alto and once for tenor saxes. The online audio is available for streaming or download using the unique code printed inside the book, and it includes **PLAYBACK+** *options such as looping and tempo adjustments.*

1. ROCK 'N' ROLL
Bony Moronie • Charlie Brown • Hand Clappin' • Honky Tonk (Parts 1 & 2) • I'm Walkin' • Lucille (You Won't Do Your Daddy's Will) • See You Later, Alligator • Shake, Rattle and Roll.
00113137 Book/Online Audio $16.99

2. R&B
Cleo's Mood • I Got a Woman • Pick up the Pieces • Respect • Shot Gun • Soul Finger • Soul Serenade • Unchain My Heart.
00113177 Book/Online Audio $16.99

3. CLASSIC ROCK
Baker Street • Deacon Blues • The Heart of Rock and Roll • Jazzman • Smooth Operator • Turn the Page • Who Can It Be Now? • Young Americans.
00113429 Book/Online Audio $16.99

4. SAX CLASSICS
Boulevard of Broken Dreams • Harlem Nocturne • Night Train • Peter Gunn • The Pink Panther • St. Thomas • Tequila • Yakety Sax.
00114393 Book/Online Audio. $16.99

5. CHARLIE PARKER
Billie's Bounce (Bill's Bounce) • Confirmation • Dewey Square • Donna Lee • Now's the Time • Ornithology • Scrapple from the Apple • Yardbird Suite.
00118286 Book/Online Audio $16.99

6. DAVE KOZ
All I See Is You • Can't Let You Go (The Sha La Song) • Emily • Honey-Dipped • Know You by Heart • Put the Top Down • Together Again • You Make Me Smile.
00118292 Book/Online Audio $16.99

7. GROVER WASHINGTON, JR.
East River Drive • Just the Two of Us • Let It Flow • Make Me a Memory (Sad Samba) • Mr. Magic • Take Five • Take Me There • Winelight.
00118293 Book/Online Audio $16.99

8. DAVID SANBORN
Anything You Want • Bang Bang • Chicago Song • Comin' Home Baby • The Dream • Hideaway • Slam • Straight to the Heart.
00125694 Book/Online Audio $16.99

9. CHRISTMAS
The Christmas Song (Chestnuts Roasting on an Open Fire) • Christmas Time Is Here • Count Your Blessings Instead of Sheep • Do You Hear What I Hear • Have Yourself a Merry Little Christmas • The Little Drummer Boy • White Christmas • Winter Wonderland.
00148170 Book/Online Audio $16.99

10. JOHN COLTRANE
Blue Train (Blue Trane) • Body and Soul • Central Park West • Cousin Mary • Giant Steps • Like Sonny (Simple Like) • My Favorite Things • Naima (Niema).
00193333 Book/Online Audio $16.99

11. JAZZ ICONS
Body and Soul • Con Alma • Oleo • Speak No Evil • Take Five • There Will Never Be Another You • Tune Up • Work Song.
00199296 Book/Online Audio $16.99

12. SMOOTH JAZZ
Bermuda Nights • Blue Water • Europa • Flirt • Love Is on the Way • Maputo • Songbird • Winelight.
00248670 Book/Online Audio $16.99

13. BONEY JAMES
Butter • Let It Go • Stone Groove • Stop, Look, Listen (To Your Heart) • Sweet Thing • Tick Tock • Total Experience • Vinyl.
00257186 Book/Online Audio $16.99

Visit Hal Leonard online at **www.halleonard.com**